How to Thrive

in 2025

How to Thrive in 2025

Simple Steps for Success, Balance and Wellbeing in Modern Life.

First published in Great Britain in 2024

Copyright © Glen Butler 2024

The moral right of the author has been asserted.

All rights reserved. Without limiting the rights under copyright reserved above, no part of this publication may be reproduced, stored or introduced into a retrieval system, or transmitted in any form or by any means (electronic, mechanical, photocopying, recording or otherwise), without the prior written permission of both the copyright owner and the publisher of this book.

ISBN: 9798343733471

How to Thrive in 2025

Simple Steps for Success, Balance, and Wellbeing in Modern Life

Glen Butler

Contents:

1. Foreword

3. Introduction

8. Chapter 1: Purpose and Meaning – The Foundation of Thriving

14. Chapter 2: Mindset Shifts - Changing the Way You Think

22. Chapter 3: Micro Habits and Consistency - The Power of Small Actions

30. Chapter 4: Systems Over Goals - Why Sustainable Success Comes from the Right Systems

38. Chapter 5: Thriving in the Digital Age - Balancing Technology and Well-being

44. Chapter 6: Resilience and Grit - The Keys to Bouncing Back and Thriving Long-Term

52. Chapter 7: Thriving in Uncertainty - Adapting to Change and Embracing the Unknown

60. Chapter 8: Playfulness and Creativity - Thriving Through Innovation and Joy

68. Chapter 9: The Power of Emotional Intelligence - Cultivating Self-Awareness and Empathy

76. Chapter 10: The Joy of Play - Building Resilience Through Fun and Experimentation

82. Chapter 11: Connection and Community - Thriving Together, Not Alone

90. Chapter 12: Redefining Success - Beyond Traditional Measures

98. Chapter 13: Thriving Through Rest and Recovery - The Importance of Switching Off

106. Chapter 14: Thriving in Relationships - Building Deeper Connections

112. Chapter 15: The Thriving Mindset - Are You Thriving or Just Coping?

120. Chapter 16: Your Roadmap to Thriving - Putting It All Together

Foreword

A Personal Challenge—Practicing What I Preach

I have to be honest: as I've been writing this book, I've faced some unexpected challenges. Here I am, diving deep into the practices that h people thrive, and I've realized I'm not exactly thriving myself. In fact, th are days when I feel like I'm doing the opposite. Staying focused, avoidii distractions, and following through without procrastinating - it's been ha than I'd like to admit.

It's ironic, really. As I go through each chapter, sharing the techniques an habits that can help people flourish, I see things I need to be doing more myself. And that's when it hit me: thriving isn't just about what you know- it's about what you do. It's easy to read good advice, but actually applying day-to-day, that's where the real challenge - and the real growth - begins.

So, here's my first message to you as you start this book: knowing isn't enough. The ideas and strategies I'm sharing here are more than just concepts to think about; they're tools to put into action. I want to encoura you not to simply read along, nodding at each idea as if it's "nice to know." I've learned firsthand that thriving is a result of actively engaging with these ideas, not just agreeing with them in theory.

My other key learning is that thriving isn't the same for everyone. Some people have lots of plans and goals that they want to achieve, others are currently seeing where life takes them. Whatever your path, your resilience will be tested in very different ways, and you'll need to take different approaches to thriving. Find what works for you, when you need it.

Make a Plan to Thrive

As you read each chapter, keep in mind that this book is designed to be a practical guide. To get the most out of it, I encourage you to make a clear action plan as you go. Identify the techniques that resonate with you and think about how you'll implement them in your daily life. Not everything needs to happen at once. Start by choosing a few strategies that feel meaningful to you and focus on those.

Here's a simple way to turn reading into action:

1. Choose What Fits: Pick the techniques that feel most valuable to you. Whether it's time-blocking, taking mindful breaks, or setting boundaries, choose what makes sense for your life right now.

2. Make an Action Plan: Write down a weekly or monthly plan for trying these tools. Commit to small steps that will help you build momentum, one day at a time.

3. Track and Reflect: Check in with yourself regularly. Are the changes you're making helping you thrive? Adjust as needed, focusing on what truly works for you.

We're in This Together

If I'm honest, this book is just as much a guide for me as it is for you. Writing it has shown me that knowing something isn't the same as applying it. So, as you begin, remember that thriving is a journey - one that requires consistent effort and self-reflection. Let's not just learn together; let's take action, make real changes, and discover what thriving looks like for each of us.

Now, let's dive in.

Introduction: Building Your Path to Thriving in 2025

What does it mean to truly thrive in 2025? The world is evolving faster than ever - technological advancements, shifting work environments, and changing societal dynamics are shaping every aspect of our lives. For many, these rapid changes can feel overwhelming, but they also offer tremendous opportunities. The secret to thriving lies in embracing these changes with a mindset that turns uncertainty into growth, challenges into opportunities, and self-doubt into confidence.

This book is about more than just surviving the changes we face; it's about thriving - building a life that is rich with purpose, joy, and resilience in the face of whatever comes next.

Thriving as a Series of Building Blocks

Success and fulfilment aren't achieved overnight, nor are they the result of mastering a single trait or mindset. Thriving is like constructing a building - brick by brick, layer by layer. That's why this book is designed with a series of building blocks, each chapter contributing a crucial element that will help you thrive in a rapidly changing world.

We start by grounding you in purpose and mindset - setting the foundation for everything that follows. Then, we'll move into practical strategies for building habits, creating systems that support your growth, and managing life in the digital age. As you progress, you'll learn how to thrive emotionally, creatively, and relationally, even in unfamiliar and challenging environments.

How This Book is Structured

Each chapter serves as a building block to help you construct your path to thriving. You'll explore how to develop a thriving mindset, build habits that sustain long-term success, and navigate uncertainty with confidence. From practical strategies to mindset shifts, this book will provide you with the tools to not just handle challenges but to grow through them.

At the midpoint, there's a chance to pause and reflect on your progress. You'll find a quiz to check your recall of key concepts, as well as journaling space titled "How Am I Thriving?" where you can capture notes on how your mindset is evolving and what new actions or behaviours you've tried so far. This reflection is essential to solidify what you've learned before moving to the next stage.

The final chapters will help you apply everything you've built - helping you thrive in relationships, adapt to new environments, and find meaning in your work and life. And at the end of the book, there will be a call to action - a roadmap that ties everything together and encourages you to keep experimenting, playing, and growing long after you finish reading.

What You'll Get Out of This Book

This book isn't about offering quick fixes or rigid formulas for success. It's about cultivating a mindset that allows you to adapt, grow, and thrive no matter what 2025 throws your way. Through practical insights, inspiring stories, and real-world examples, you'll learn how to:

- Find and live your purpose.
- Build micro habits that lead to big changes.
- Balance life in the digital age without burning out.
- Use creativity and playfulness to solve problems and stay innovative.
- Cultivate resilience and grit to bounce back from setbacks.
- Thrive in new environments, whether it's a new job, a foreign country, or a challenging situation.
- Build strong, thriving relationships.

The goal isn't just to give you a roadmap for 2025 but to help you build a thriving mindset for the rest of your life. Each chapter will link directly to the next, showing you how to layer these insights together to build the life you want.

Thriving Isn't Just About Success - It's About Enjoying the Journey

Thriving in 2025 isn't just about working harder or doing more. It's about enjoying the process, staying playful, and being curious about what's possible. You'll be challenged to experiment, practice, and have fun along the way. After all, thriving is as much about the joy of discovery as it is about achieving goals.

So, let's begin. Whether you're here to rewire your mindset, cultivate new habits, or redefine success, this book will be your guide. Together, we'll lay the foundation, block by block, to help you thrive in 2025 - and far beyond.

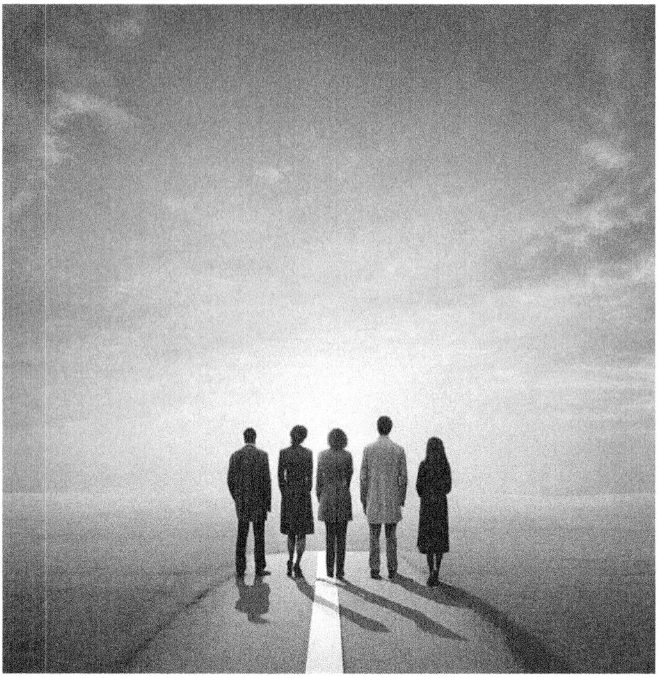

Chapter 1: Purpose and Meaning - The Foundation of Thriving

To thrive, we need to know why we do what we do. Purpose gives us direction, motivation, and the energy to keep going when things get tough. In 2025, with the constant noise, distractions, and ever-growing pressures of modern life, finding and holding onto a clear sense of purpose is more important than ever.

Purpose isn't just about setting goals or achieving ambitions; it's about meaning. It's the core reason behind our actions and choices - the force that pulls us forward when everything else feels overwhelming. Without a clear sense of purpose, even success can feel empty and unfulfilling. But when you connect with your purpose, you find a deeper drive that transforms surviving into thriving.

As author and motivational expert Dan Pink highlights, motivation is fuelled by three key elements: autonomy, mastery, and purpose. Purpose is the most powerful of these because it taps into our intrinsic desire to make a meaningful impact. It gives us a reason to persevere, to grow, and to align our daily actions with a greater sense of meaning. This is why establishing a strong sense of purpose is the first building block to thriving in 2025.

Why Purpose Matters

The power of purpose has been studied extensively in psychology. People with a clear sense of purpose are more resilient, happier, and fulfilled. When faced with setbacks, they bounce back faster because they're anchored in something bigger than themselves. Purpose transforms obstacles into challenges worth tackling and creates a sense of alignment in everything you do.

Viktor Frankl, a Holocaust survivor and psychiatrist, famously wrote in *Man's Search for Meaning*, "Those who have a 'why' to live, can bear with almost any 'how.'" His experiences in the Nazi concentration camps taught him that having a sense of purpose was key to survival. For Frankl, and for all of us, purpose gives life meaning—even in the face of unimaginable hardship.

Most of us will never face conditions as extreme as Frankl's, but we all encounter challenges - whether it's work stress, relationship struggles, health issues, or financial difficulties. Having a strong sense of purpose can help us rise above these challenges, providing the resilience and focus to keep moving forward.

The Link Between Purpose and Motivation

Dan Pink argues that purpose is one of the key drivers of motivation because it connects our actions to something meaningful. When you're clear about your purpose, tasks that might otherwise feel mundane or frustrating suddenly have value. Purpose acts as the "why" behind our efforts, making even difficult moments worthwhile.

Pink's model also emphasizes autonomy (the freedom to make choices) and mastery (the drive to improve). Together with purpose, these elements form the foundation of lasting motivation. When you have autonomy over your goals, are working toward mastery in your craft, and are driven by a clear purpose, you unlock the energy to thrive.

The Story of Howard Schultz: Purpose in Action

A great example of purpose in action is Howard Schultz, the former CEO of Starbucks. Schultz's journey with Starbucks wasn't just about building a profitable company - it was driven by a deeper purpose. In the early 1980s, during a trip to Italy, Schultz was struck by the culture of community surrounding Italian espresso bars. They weren't just places to grab coffee - they were gathering spaces where people connected, relaxed, and conversed.

When Schultz returned to the U.S., he had a vision: to create a similar experience in America. His purpose was to build more than a chain of coffee shops; he wanted to create spaces where people could come together and feel a sense of belonging. This purpose became the driving force behind Starbucks' success. Schultz wasn't just selling coffee - he was fulfilling a mission that sustained the company through challenges and fuelled its rapid growth.

For Schultz, purpose turned a simple business into a global movement. It guided his decisions, inspired his leadership, and created a culture that resonated with employees and customers alike. That's the power of purpose: it transforms ordinary tasks into meaningful actions and aligns people with a shared vision.

Finding Your Purpose: Your Personal 'Why'

So how do you find your own purpose? It starts with self-reflection and asking the right questions:

- What motivates me to get up in the morning?
- What are the activities or causes that energize me?
- What kind of legacy do I want to leave behind?
- How can my strengths and passions make a positive impact on the world or those around me?

Your purpose doesn't have to be grand or world changing. It can be as simple as dedicating yourself to being a great parent, contributing positively to your community, or pursuing a career that aligns with your values. What matters is that your purpose resonates deeply with you and gives you a sense of meaning and direction.

Exercise: Write Your Purpose Statement

Take a moment to reflect on your life. What drives you? What brings you the most meaning? Based on your reflections, write a purpose statement - a short, clear sentence or two that encapsulates your core purpose. This statement will serve as an anchor throughout the rest of this book, helping you stay grounded as you navigate life's challenges.

Examples of purpose statements:

- "My purpose is to use my creativity to inspire and connect with others."

- "I strive to support and nurture the people I care about, bringing joy and stability into their lives."
- "My purpose is to make a positive impact on the environment through my work and lifestyle choices."

Revisit your purpose statement regularly. Use it to check in with yourself - are your daily actions aligned with your purpose? If not, what small changes can you make to reconnect with your 'why'?

Adapting Your Purpose in a Changing World

In 2025, the world will look different. Jobs will evolve, technology will continue to advance, and the way we live, and work will keep shifting. Your purpose, however, can be your constant guide. The more grounded you are in your purpose, the more adaptable you'll be in the face of change.

Purpose acts as a compass, helping you cut through distractions and stay focused on what truly matters. When you're connected to your purpose, external changes don't knock you off course - they become opportunities to refine and deepen your sense of meaning.

The Benefits of Living with Purpose

Research shows that people with a clear sense of purpose tend to live longer, healthier, and more fulfilling lives. Purpose is linked to better mental health, greater life satisfaction, and even physical well-being. When you have a reason to get up in the morning, you're more likely to engage in healthy behaviours, build strong relationships, and pursue meaningful goals.

Living with purpose also reduces stress and anxiety. Instead of feeling overwhelmed by life's demands, people with purpose see challenges as opportunities to grow. They experience greater control over their lives because their actions are aligned with their values.

Key Takeaways

- Purpose is foundational to thriving in 2025—it gives your life direction, energy, and meaning.

- Dan Pink's framework shows how purpose, autonomy, and mastery drive lasting motivation.

- Howard Schultz's purpose-driven vision for Starbucks transformed his business into a global movement.

- Living with purpose makes you more resilient, adaptable, and fulfilled, especially in a rapidly changing world.

- Your purpose can evolve over time, but staying connected to your 'why' will keep you grounded no matter what life throws your way.

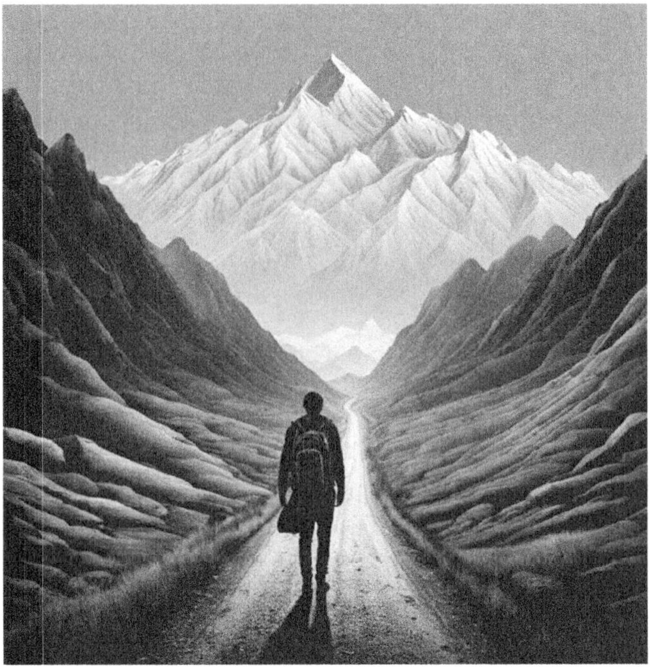

Chapter 2: Mindset Shifts - Changing the Way You Think

If thriving is the goal, mindset is the fuel that powers everything. The way you think shapes your entire experience of life - how you handle challenges, pursue goals, and interact with others. In 2025, with the pace of change faster than ever, your mindset will be the key to adapting, growing, and thriving.

Thriving in 2025 requires letting go of old, self-defeating beliefs and embracing new ways of thinking. But the challenge many people face is they often think they're thriving when, in reality, they're simply coping. They're busy, working hard, and ticking all the boxes, but inside they feel disconnected, unfulfilled, or burned out.

This chapter will explore how mindset shifts can help you break free from survival mode and start thriving. By changing how you see yourself, your work, and your challenges, you can build a mindset that sets the foundation for lasting growth and fulfilment.

Here's a short activity to prove the importance of your mindset. Set a timer on your phone for 1 minute. As you start it, you now have 60 seconds to look around you and see how many red items you can see in the room you're in. Make a mental note of each one as you'll be tested on them in a moment. Now, go, start that timer!

Have you done it? Great!

Now without looking around you, make a list of all the blue items you have just noticed in your room...

How many were you able to recall?

This is a simple activity that I have used in many training sessions to demonstrate that when our minds are focused on looking for something, it's incredibly easy to miss so much else.

Your mindset makes all the difference.

Thriving beyond the surface

One of the most common traps people fall into is mistaking busyness or external success for thriving. You've just been promoted at work, your schedule is packed with meetings, social events, and projects, and you feel like you're achieving something. But despite being productive, you're still left with a feeling that something is missing. You're getting things done, but you're not connected to a deeper sense of purpose or joy. That's not thriving - that's coping with the pressures of life, and it's a cycle many of us get stuck in.

James Blunt offers a great example of how mindset can shift your response to external criticism or pressure. After the massive success of his song "You're Beautiful," the track became overplayed, and a wave of public backlash followed. Instead of letting the criticism defeat him or retreating into silence, Blunt decided to embrace the situation with humour. On Twitter, instead of ignoring negative comments, he responded with witty, sarcastic, and sometimes rude replies that transformed the narrative. His resilience and ability to laugh at himself not only disarmed his critics but also won him a new wave of fans who appreciated his authenticity. Blunt's story shows us that mindset is everything - it can turn external criticism into an opportunity for humour, connection, and growth.

Blunt's approach teaches us that thriving isn't about avoiding challenges or criticism; it's about how you choose to respond. Your mindset can transform obstacles into opportunities for growth, connection, or even laughter.

The Fixed vs. Growth Mindset

One of the most powerful mindset shifts you can make is moving from a fixed mindset to a growth mindset. Coined by psychologist Carol Dweck, these terms describe two fundamentally different ways of thinking about your abilities and potential.

In a fixed mindset, you believe that your talents, intelligence, and personality traits are set in stone. You might think, "I'm just not good at public speaking" or "I'm not creative." When you encounter challenges or setbacks, a fixed mindset sees them as evidence of your limitations. This mindset is limiting because it discourages risk-taking and stops you from pushing yourself outside of your comfort zone.

On the other hand, a growth mindset embraces the idea that your abilities and intelligence can be developed through effort, learning, and perseverance. People with a growth mindset see challenges as opportunities to learn and improve. Instead of thinking, "I'm not good at this," they think, "I'm not good at this *yet* - but I can get better with practice."

Arnold Schwarzenegger is a prime example of someone who thrived through a growth mindset. When he arrived in the United States, his accent, physique, and background as a bodybuilder were seen as barriers to becoming a movie star. Many told him he would never make it in Hollywood. But instead of accepting those limitations, Schwarzenegger saw them as challenges. He used his unique appearance and accent to his advantage, turning what others saw as obstacles into strengths. His growth mindset allowed him to adapt, persist, and thrive in an industry where few thought he could succeed.

How to Shift Your Mindset

Shifting your mindset isn't an overnight process, but with conscious effort, you can start to reshape the way you think about challenges, growth, and success. Here are a few practical ways to cultivate a thriving mindset:

1. Reframe Challenges as Opportunities

Whenever you face a challenge, ask yourself: "How can I grow from this?" Instead of viewing setbacks as failures, see them as opportunities to learn something new or strengthen a skill. This shift in perspective helps you stay motivated and engaged, even when things aren't going perfectly.

Take James Blunt's example. Instead of letting negative comments get under his skin, he used them as fuel for witty, clever responses that reshaped the public perception of him. Blunt's ability to turn criticism into an opportunity for humour shows the power of reframing challenges.

2. Embrace Effort and Persistence

A growth mindset values effort and persistence. Instead of believing that success should come easily if you're talented, recognise that effort is part of the process. When things get difficult, remind yourself that growth often comes through struggle. Effort is not a sign of weakness - it's a sign that you're pushing beyond your current limits.

Look at Arnold Schwarzenegger's story. He didn't let early rejection stop him. His persistence and belief that he could learn, adapt, and grow eventually led him to become a global superstar, politician, and entrepreneur. Schwarzenegger's success was built on the foundation of relentless effort and perseverance.

3. Practice Self-Compassion

Thriving isn't about being perfect - it's about progress. Along the way, you'll make mistakes, encounter setbacks, and face challenges that test your resilience. When this happens, it's important to practice self-compassion. Be kind to yourself in moments of failure, and remind yourself that growth takes time.

Self-compassion is especially important in 2025, where the pressure to constantly achieve and keep up with others can lead to burnout. Instead of being your own harshest critic, shift your mindset to one of compassion and patience. This allows you to recover from setbacks more quickly and continue moving forward with greater resilience.

Practical Exercise: Reframing Your Mindset

Now that you understand the difference between a fixed and growth mindset, it's time to put it into practice. Think about an area of your life where you've felt stuck or defeated. Maybe it's a work challenge, a personal goal, or a skill you've been struggling to master.

1. Write down the current belief or mindset you have about this challenge. For example, you might write, "I'll never be able to learn this new software - it's too complicated."

2. Next, rewrite this belief from a growth mindset perspective. For example: "Learning this software is difficult now, but with time and practice, I can get better at it."
3. Commit to practising this new mindset over the next week. Each time you face the challenge, remind yourself of your growth mindset belief.

Over time, these small mindset shifts will accumulate and help you approach challenges with greater optimism, resilience, and curiosity.

The Power of Mindset in Thriving

Your mindset shapes how you experience life. It determines whether you see obstacles as barriers or as opportunities, whether you stay stuck or move forward. By making small shifts in the way you think, you can transform your approach to challenges and set yourself on the path to thriving.

In 2025, the ability to adapt and grow will be more important than ever. Life will continue to throw curveballs, but with a thriving mindset, you'll have the resilience and flexibility to rise to any challenge. Whether you're facing criticism, adapting to new environments, or pushing yourself out of your comfort zone, your mindset will be the key to thriving in an ever-changing world.

Key Takeaways:

- Mindset is everything - it shapes how you perceive challenges, success, and growth.

- James Blunt's humorous responses to public criticism show how mindset can turn challenges into opportunities.

- A growth mindset allows you to see challenges as opportunities for learning and improvement, rather than fixed limitations.

- Shifting your mindset involves reframing challenges, embracing effort, and practising self-compassion.

- Arnold Schwarzenegger's career is a testament to the power of persistence, adaptability, and a thriving mindset.

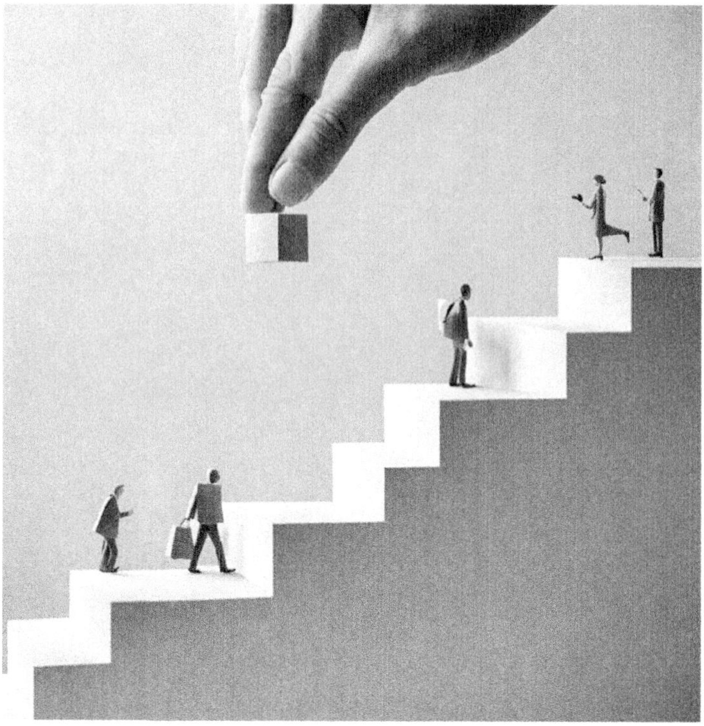

Chapter 3: Micro Habits and Consistency - The Power of Small Actions

When we think about thriving, it's easy to imagine big leaps forward - major successes, life-changing moments, or dramatic transformations. But the reality is that thriving comes from the small, consistent actions we take every day. In the fast-paced world of 2025, where life feels busier and more chaotic than ever, micro habits offer a practical way to make lasting change without feeling overwhelmed.

A micro habit is a small, easily achievable action that, when done consistently, can lead to significant long-term results. It's not about making radical changes overnight, but about committing to small, repeatable behaviours that gradually compound into major improvements. The beauty of micro habits lies in their simplicity - because they're so small, they're easy to stick with, even in the busiest of schedules.

In this chapter, we'll explore the power of micro habits and how consistency—more than intensity—creates real, sustainable progress. By the end, you'll see how incorporating tiny actions into your daily routine can have a transformative impact on your ability to thrive in 2025 and beyond.

Why Micro Habits Work

The science behind micro habits is simple: when a behaviour is small and achievable, it's less intimidating, and you're more likely to stick with it. Micro habits also avoid the common pitfalls of willpower and motivation. We often fail to achieve our goals because we set them too big or too vague. But a micro habit is so easy, it requires almost no effort, which means you can do it even on the days when you're tired, stressed, or unmotivated.

James Clear, author of *Atomic Habits*, explains that micro habits allow us to take advantage of the compound effect - the idea that small, consistent actions lead to significant long-term gains. Just as compound interest grows your money over time, micro habits grow your success. Whether it's reading one page a day, doing two push-ups every morning, or writing for just five minutes, the key is consistency.

The Power of Consistency Over Intensity

Most people think that big results come from big efforts. But thriving isn't about intense bursts of effort - it's about consistency over time. Small, steady actions may not feel significant in the moment, but over weeks, months, and years, they build momentum and lead to massive results.

Think about training for a marathon. If you try to run 10 miles on your first day of training, you'll likely burn out quickly. But if you start by running half a mile a day, gradually increasing your distance over time, you'll build the endurance needed to complete the marathon. The same principle applies to any goal - whether it's learning a new skill, improving your fitness, or developing a daily routine that supports your mental and emotional health.

This is where micro habits shine. Because they're small, they're easy to do consistently. And because they're done consistently, they create long-term change.

Stephen King: The Power of Daily Habits

One of the most prolific writers of our time, Stephen King, attributes much of his success to small, consistent habits. King doesn't wait for inspiration to strike - he shows up every day to write. His daily habit of writing a set number of words has resulted in over 60 published novels, with many of them becoming bestsellers. King understands that success isn't about writing a masterpiece in one sitting - it's about the cumulative power of daily effort.

King's writing routine is a perfect example of the power of micro habits. By writing just a little bit every day, he has built a body of work that spans decades. His success didn't come from dramatic bursts of creativity, but from the consistency of sitting down to write every single day.

This shows us that thriving isn't about one big moment of effort - it's about the steady accumulation of small actions over time. Whether your goal is to write a book, run a marathon, or improve your health, consistency is the key to making lasting progress.

Why Micro Habits Are Perfect for Busy Lives

One of the biggest challenges people face when trying to build new habits is the feeling of being too busy. In 2025, when our lives are packed with work, family commitments, and the constant pull of digital distractions, it's easy to feel like there's no time to focus on personal growth or well-being. But that's where micro habits come in - they're so small that they can fit into even the busiest of schedules.

For example, if your goal is to get fit, you don't need to spend an hour at the gym every day. Instead, start with a micro habit like doing two push-ups every morning. Two push-ups take less than 30 seconds, so it's impossible to claim you don't have time for them. Once you've mastered the habit of doing two push-ups, you can gradually increase the number or add other exercises. The important thing is that you're building consistency.

In a world where time feels like a scarce resource, micro habits offer a way to make progress without requiring huge chunks of time. They fit seamlessly into your daily routine and create a sense of accomplishment, even on the busiest days.

The Compound Effect: How Small Habits Add Up

The real magic of micro habits is in the compound effect - the idea that small, consistent actions add up over time to produce significant results. Think of it like planting a seed. At first, it's just a tiny sprout, barely noticeable. But with regular watering and care, it grows into a strong, flourishing plant.

The same principle applies to habits. Doing one push-up today won't make much difference, but doing one push-up every day for a year will. Reading one page of a book today won't make you a literary expert, but reading one page a day for a year will add up to 365 pages - roughly a full-length book. The key is consistency. Over time, the small actions compound, and their impact becomes significant.

The Power of Identity-Based Habits

One of the most effective ways to make micro habits stick is to tie them to your identity. Instead of focusing solely on the outcome you want to achieve, think about the kind of person you want to become. When your habits are aligned with your identity, they become more meaningful and easier to maintain.

For example, if you want to start running, don't just set a goal of running a certain number of miles. Instead, start thinking of yourself as a runner. When you identify as a runner, running becomes part of who you are, not just something you do. Even if you're only running a short distance each day, the habit reinforces your identity as a runner, making it more likely that you'll stick with it.

This identity-based approach can be applied to any habit. If you want to write more, think of yourself as a writer, even if you're only writing a few sentences a day. If you want to improve your health, see yourself as someone who prioritises well-being, even if your micro habit is as small as drinking an extra glass of water each day.

By focusing on the kind of person you want to become, your micro habits take on more significance, and you're more likely to stay consistent.

How to Create Effective Micro Habits

Creating effective micro habits is simple, but it requires a bit of planning. Here's how to get started:

1. Start Small

The key to micro habits is to start small - so small that the habit feels almost effortless. The smaller the habit, the more likely you are to stick with it. For example, if your goal is to meditate, don't start with 20 minutes of meditation a day. Start with just one minute. Once you've built consistency with one minute, you can gradually increase the time.

2. Make It Specific

Vague habits like "exercise more" or "eat healthier" are hard to stick to because they're not specific. Instead, be clear about what your micro habit will look like. For example, "do two push-ups every morning" or "eat one piece of fruit with lunch" are specific, actionable habits that you can easily track.

3. Tie It to an Existing Routine

One of the best ways to make micro habits stick is to tie them to an existing routine. This technique, known as "habit stacking," helps you remember to do the new habit because it's connected to something you already do. For example, if you want to start flossing, tie it to your existing habit of brushing your teeth. After brushing, you automatically floss.

4. Track Your Progress

Tracking your micro habits can help you stay consistent and motivated. Use a habit tracker or simply mark off a calendar each time you complete your habit. The act of checking off a day gives you a sense of accomplishment and reinforces the habit.

5. Focus on Consistency, Not Perfection

The goal of micro habits is consistency, not perfection. It's okay if you miss a day—what's important is that you get back on track the next day. Don't let one missed day derail your progress. The power of micro habits lies in their ability to keep you moving forward, even in small steps.

Practical Exercise: Start a Micro Habit

Now it's time to put the power of micro habits into action. Think about an area of your life where you'd like to make progress - whether it's fitness, learning a new skill, improving your mental health, or becoming more productive.

1. **Choose a micro habit**: Pick a habit that's so small it feels almost effortless. For example, if you want to start reading more, commit to

reading one page a day. If you want to start exercising, commit to doing one push-up a day.

2. **Make it specific**: Write down your micro habit in clear, actionable terms. For example, "I will read one page of a book every night before bed" or "I will do one push-up every morning after brushing my teeth."

3. **Track your progress**: Use a habit tracker or calendar to mark off each day you complete your habit. Celebrate your consistency, no matter how small the action feels.

Key Takeaways:

- Thriving comes from small, consistent actions rather than dramatic changes.
- Sustainable growth happens by showing up regularly, not through short bursts of effort.
- Small habits add up over time, creating meaningful results in the long run.
- Micro habits fit easily into busy schedules, making personal growth more achievable.
- Aligning habits with the person you want to become makes them more meaningful.
- Tying new habits to existing routines helps make them automatic and easier to remember.
- Celebrate consistency, even if progress feels small, and focus on staying on track.
- Stephen King's daily writing routine shows how steady efforts can lead to great success.
- Micro habits are flexible and can evolve as you grow, helping you build on your progress.

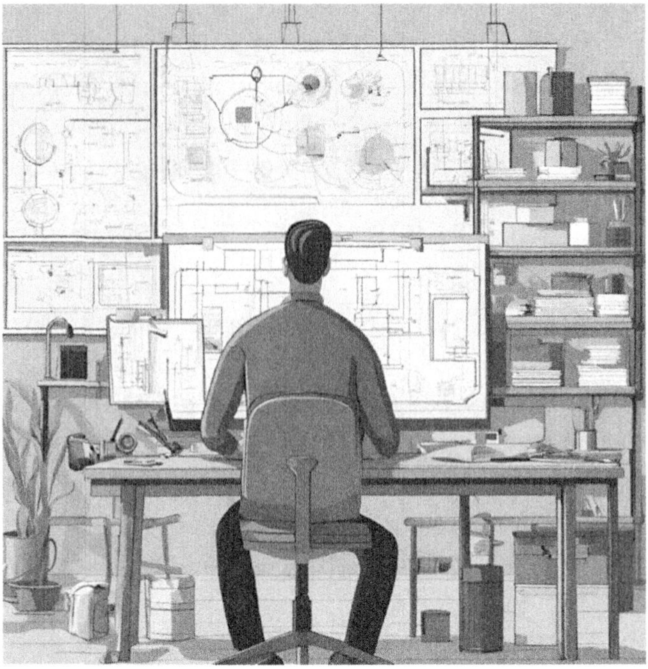

Chapter 4: Systems Over Goals - Why Sustainable Success Comes from the Right Systems

Goals are great - they give us direction and motivation. But as many people have experienced, setting goals is one thing; achieving them is another. In fact, focusing solely on goals can sometimes lead to burnout, frustration, and even failure. That's because goals are often outcome-focused, and they rely on motivation and willpower, which can wane over time.

In contrast, systems are the repeatable processes or habits that lead to achieving those goals. Systems are about the daily actions, routines, and frameworks that you put in place to make progress, even when motivation dips. Thriving in 2025 means creating systems that not only help you achieve your goals but also ensure that your success is sustainable over the long term.

In this chapter, we'll explore why systems are more powerful than goals, how to create effective systems in your life, and how focusing on systems can help you thrive in 2025.

The Problem with Relying Solely on Goals

We've all set ambitious goals at some point - whether it's losing weight, learning a new skill, or hitting a career milestone. But after the initial excitement fades, the reality sets in: goals require consistent effort, and without the right systems in place, that effort can quickly become unsustainable. That's where many people get stuck.

Let's take the example of someone who sets a goal to run a marathon. The goal is specific, measurable, and time-bound—all great qualities for a goal. But without a clear plan or system to achieve it, that goal can quickly feel overwhelming. The runner might start out strong, but without a structured training routine, the goal becomes harder to achieve as motivation dwindles or life gets in the way.

The problem isn't the goal itself - it's the lack of a system to support it.

Systems vs. Goals: What's the Difference?

Goals are the results you want to achieve - finish a marathon, write a book, lose 10 pounds, or get a promotion. They focus on the end point. While goals are important for setting direction, they can create unnecessary pressure, and failure to meet them can feel disheartening. Additionally, once a goal is achieved, you're often left thinking, "What next?"

Systems, on the other hand, focus on the process. A system is a set of repeatable actions or habits that you perform regularly, regardless of the outcome. When you focus on systems, you're not fixated on the end result - you're more concerned with the daily actions that will eventually lead to success.

For example, instead of focusing solely on the goal of running a marathon, a system would involve creating a consistent weekly training schedule: running three times a week, gradually increasing your distance, and incorporating rest days. This system ensures that you're making progress, even on the days when motivation is low. And the beauty of systems is that they're sustainable—once the marathon is over, the system you've built can continue to support your fitness journey.

Scott Adams: Systems Beat Goals Every Time

Scott Adams, the creator of the famous comic strip *Dilbert*, is a big advocate for focusing on systems rather than goals. In his book *How to Fail at Almost Everything and Still Win Big*, Adams explains that focusing on systems is what helped him succeed, even when he faced multiple failures early in his career.

Adams makes the point that goals are often limiting because they create a binary scenario: either you achieve the goal, or you don't. If you don't, it can feel like a failure. But with a system, success isn't measured by whether or not you've reached the finish line - it's about whether you're consistently making progress. Adams attributes much of his success to the systems he put in place, such as his daily writing routine, which led to the creation of *Dilbert*.

By focusing on the process rather than the end result, Adams was able to build a successful career, even when his initial goals didn't pan out. Systems allow for adaptability and growth, while goals can feel rigid and limiting.

The Benefits of a System-Focused Approach

Focusing on systems has several key advantages over a goal-oriented approach:

1. Consistency is Key

When you focus on systems, you're not relying on bursts of motivation or willpower. Instead, you're building consistent habits that lead to long-term success. Motivation is fleeting, but systems create structure and routine, which keeps you moving forward even when motivation fades.

2. Flexibility and Adaptability

Goals can feel rigid and unyielding, which makes it harder to adapt when circumstances change. Systems, on the other hand, are flexible. If something isn't working, you can tweak the system without abandoning your progress. This adaptability is essential in a fast-paced world like 2025, where the ability to pivot is often the key to thriving.

3. Reduces Pressure and Anxiety

Focusing solely on goals can create a lot of pressure - especially if the goal feels distant or difficult to achieve. Systems reduce this pressure by shifting your focus from the outcome to the process. As long as you're following the system, you're making progress, and that's what matters.

4. Creates Momentum

Once a system is in place, it creates momentum. Over time, the actions become automatic, and you no longer need to rely on motivation to get things done. This momentum builds over time, leading to bigger and better results than you could achieve by simply setting goals.

Serena Williams: A System for Success

Tennis legend Serena Williams is another great example of someone who has thrived because of her systems. Throughout her career, Williams has relied on a rigorous training system that focuses not just on preparing for specific tournaments, but on maintaining peak physical and mental fitness year-round.

Williams' system involves daily practice, strength training, nutrition, and mental preparation. This system has allowed her to stay at the top of her game for decades. Even when she's not actively competing, the system ensures that she's constantly improving and ready for the next challenge. Her focus on systems rather than just goals has given her the longevity and resilience to continue competing at an elite level.

Williams' success shows that the key to thriving isn't just setting big goals - it's building a system that supports continuous growth and improvement, regardless of whether you're currently winning or losing.

How to Build Effective Systems

Now that we've seen the power of systems, let's look at how you can build systems in your own life. The key is to focus on creating processes that are repeatable, sustainable, and adaptable. Here's how to get started:

1. Identify the Area of Your Life You Want to Improve

Start by thinking about a specific area of your life where you want to see progress. It could be related to your health, career, personal growth, or relationships. For example, you might want to improve your fitness, become more productive at work, or spend more quality time with your family.

2. Break It Down into Daily or Weekly Actions

Once you've identified the area, break it down into small, manageable actions that you can do consistently. If your goal is to improve your fitness, your system might involve exercising for 30 minutes, three times a week. If your goal is to be more productive, your system might involve blocking out time each day for focused work without distractions.

3. Focus on Consistency, Not Perfection

The key to a successful system is consistency, not perfection. It's okay to miss a day or adjust your system as needed. The important thing is that you're following a repeatable process that moves you closer to your desired outcome.

4. Track Your Progress

While systems are focused on the process, it's still important to track your progress to ensure that your system is working. Keep a journal, use a habit tracker, or simply make notes about how well your system is functioning. If something isn't working, adjust the system until it does.

5. Be Flexible and Adapt

Life is unpredictable, and your system should be flexible enough to adapt to changing circumstances. If you find that your system isn't working as well as it once did, don't be afraid to tweak it. The beauty of systems is that they can evolve over time to suit your changing needs.

Practical Exercise: Create a System

Let's put the power of systems into action. Think about a goal you've been trying to achieve but have struggled with. Now, instead of focusing on the goal itself, create a system that will help you make progress consistently.

1. **Identify your goal**: What is it that you want to achieve? For example, "I want to run a marathon" or "I want to write a book."

2. **Design a system**: Break the goal down into daily or weekly actions that will help you make progress. For example, "I will run three times a week for 30 minutes" or "I will write 500 words every day."

3. **Focus on the process**: Commit to following the system, regardless of whether you feel motivated. The key is to focus on consistency.

4. **Track and adjust**: After a few weeks, evaluate how well the system is working. If something isn't working, adjust the system rather than abandoning it altogether.

Key Takeaways:

- Goals focus on outcomes, while systems focus on the process.
- Focusing on systems creates consistency, reduces pressure, and builds momentum.
- Scott Adams and Serena Williams thrived because of their systems, not just their goals.
- Building systems involves creating repeatable, sustainable actions that support long-term success.
- Consistency, flexibility, and adaptability are key to thriving in 2025.

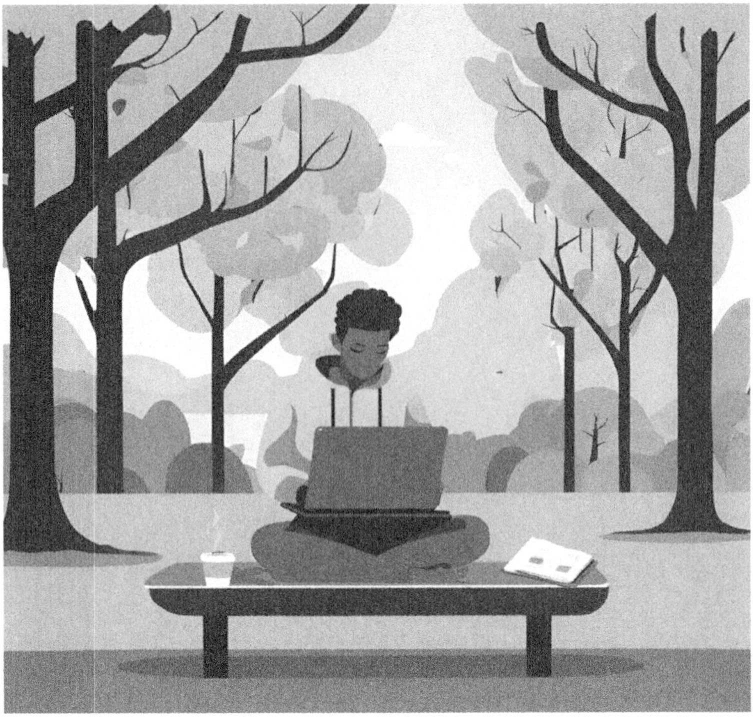

Chapter 5: Thriving in the Digital Age - Balancing Technology and Well-being

We live in an era where technology is deeply intertwined with our daily lives. From smartphones to social media, from work emails to entertainment streaming, technology is a constant presence. While these tools have undoubtedly made our lives more convenient and connected, they also pose new challenges - distractions, information overload, and the blurring of boundaries between work and personal life.

To thrive in 2025, it's essential to strike a balance between embracing the benefits of technology and maintaining your mental, emotional, and physical well-being. Technology should be a tool that helps you thrive, not a trap that drains your energy, focus, or sense of purpose.

In this chapter, we'll explore practical ways to manage technology in a way that enhances your life, rather than detracts from it. By learning to set boundaries, embrace mindfulness, and be intentional about your tech use, you can thrive in the digital age without feeling overwhelmed.

The Double-Edged Sword of Technology

There's no denying the advantages technology brings. It allows us to stay connected with people across the globe, access vast amounts of information at our fingertips, and perform tasks more efficiently than ever before. But there's also a darker side: technology can be addictive, distracting, and draining.

Think about it: How often do you find yourself mindlessly scrolling through social media, watching videos, or checking emails long after work hours have ended? These behaviours can erode your productivity, sap your energy, and make it harder to truly relax and disconnect. When left unchecked, excessive technology use can lead to stress, anxiety, and even burnout.

In 2025, the ability to balance technology with your overall well-being will be critical. Instead of letting technology dictate how you spend your time and attention, you need to take control of your relationship with it.

Cal Newport: The Power of Digital Minimalism

One person who has studied the impact of technology on our lives is Cal Newport, author of *Digital Minimalism*. Newport advocates for a more intentional approach to technology, where we carefully choose which digital tools we engage with and how we use them.

In his book, Newport argues that many of us have become passive consumers of technology, letting social media platforms, apps, and notifications dictate how we spend our time. He calls for a shift toward digital minimalism - a philosophy of using technology deliberately, in ways that align with your values and enhance your life, rather than distract from it.

Digital minimalism is about making conscious choices about how and when you use technology. For example, instead of being glued to your phone every time you have a spare moment, you might choose to set specific times for checking emails or browsing social media. This approach reduces the constant interruptions and helps you regain control over your time and attention.

Newport's approach can be a powerful tool for thriving in the digital age. By cutting back on unnecessary distractions, you create more space for meaningful work, deep connections, and intentional living.

The Boundaries Between Work and Home Are Blurring

One of the biggest challenges of the digital age is the blurred line between work and personal life, especially for those working from home. While remote work offers flexibility, it also means that the boundaries between work and home can become fuzzy.

Many people find themselves starting work earlier, working later, and not taking breaks throughout the day. Without the physical separation of an office, the workday can bleed into evenings, weekends, and even holidays. You might even find yourself checking emails or responding to messages during dinner or while relaxing on the sofa.

This lack of clear boundaries not only impacts your productivity, but it also makes it harder to switch off mentally. Instead of fully recharging during your downtime, your mind stays in work mode, leading to mental fatigue and

decision fatigue - a psychological phenomenon where the more decisions you make throughout the day, the harder it becomes to make thoughtful choices.

Batch Processing: A New Approach to Managing Your Focus

One effective way to stay productive and reduce distractions is through batch processing - grouping similar tasks together and completing them in focused blocks of time. This approach reduces the mental strain of constant context-switching, which happens when you jump from one type of task to another (e.g., answering emails, writing a report, and attending a virtual meeting).

How Batch Processing Works:

- **Group Similar Tasks Together:** Set aside specific blocks of time for similar tasks, such as responding to emails, making phone calls, or conducting research.//
- **Minimise Interruptions:** During these blocks, eliminate distractions by turning off notifications or using "Do Not Disturb" modes.
- **Schedule Intentional Breaks:** After each batch, take a short break to recharge before moving on to the next block of tasks.

By concentrating on one category of work at a time, batch processing helps you focus deeply, work more efficiently, and reduce mental fatigue caused by constant multitasking.

Jack Dorsey: Using Technology as a Tool, Not a Trap

Jack Dorsey, co-founder of Twitter and Square, is another example of someone who has found ways to balance technology use with well-being. Despite being the CEO of two major tech companies, Dorsey is known for his minimalist approach to technology in his personal life.

Dorsey structures his day with clear routines, including time for meditation, exercise, and reflection. He uses technology as a tool to enhance his work and life, but he's also mindful of how it can become a distraction. By setting clear boundaries and prioritising his well-being, Dorsey has been able to maintain high performance while avoiding the burnout that often comes with being constantly connected.

Dorsey's example shows that even in the tech industry, where being online 24/7 is the norm, it's possible to thrive by being intentional about how you use technology.

Practical Exercise: Create Your Own Digital Boundaries

To thrive in the digital age, it's important to take control of your relationship with technology. Here's a practical exercise to help you set boundaries and become more intentional about your tech use:

1. **Audit Your Tech Use:** Spend a day tracking how much time you spend on different devices and apps. Be honest with yourself - how much time is spent on productive activities, and how much is spent on mindless scrolling or checking notifications?

2. **Set Clear Tech-Free Times:** Choose specific times of day when you'll unplug from technology. For example, you might decide to disconnect during meals, after 8 PM, or for the first hour of your morning. Use this time to engage in offline activities that recharge you.

3. **Designate Tech-Free Zones:** Identify areas of your home where technology won't be used. This might include your bedroom, dining table, or living room. By creating spaces that are free from screens, you can foster more meaningful connections and relaxation.

4. **Try Batch Processing:** Group similar tasks into focused blocks of time to minimise distractions and improve productivity. For example, dedicate one block to emails, another to meetings, and another to deep work.

Key Takeaways:

- Technology is a powerful tool, but it can also be a source of distraction, stress, and burnout if not managed intentionally.

- Cal Newport's concept of digital minimalism encourages us to use technology deliberately, aligning it with our values and goals.

- Setting clear boundaries between work and personal life is essential for maintaining well-being in the digital age.

- Batch processing can help you manage your tasks and stay productive while reducing mental fatigue.

- Jack Dorsey's minimalist approach to technology shows that even in the tech industry, it's possible to maintain balance by setting clear routines and prioritising well-being.

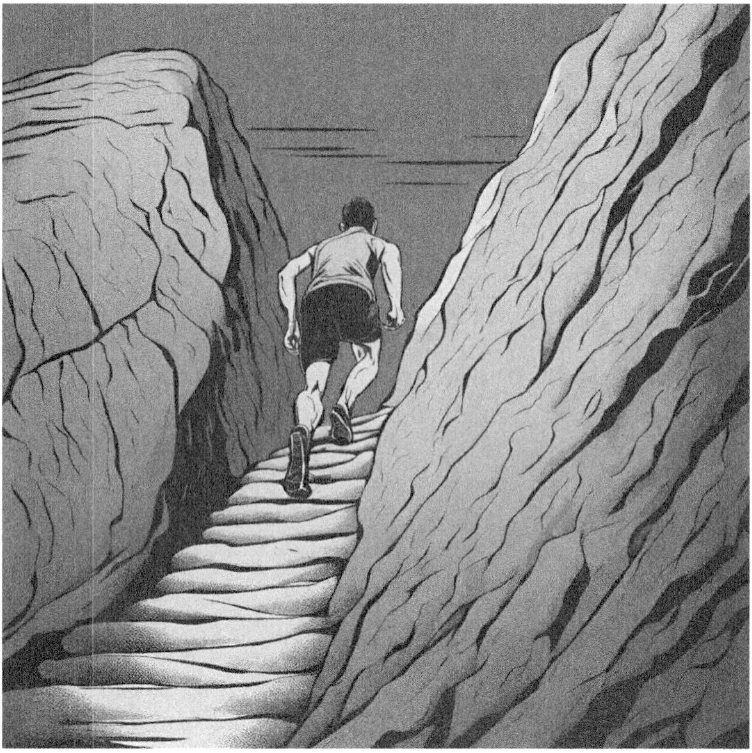

Chapter 6: Resilience and Grit - The Keys to Bouncing Back and Thriving Long-Term

Life is full of challenges. Whether it's a setback at work, a personal loss, or a sudden shift in circumstances, we all face moments where we're tested. In 2025, the ability to bounce back from these challenges and persist through adversity will be crucial. That's where resilience and grit come in.

Resilience is the ability to recover from setbacks, while grit is the determination to keep going, even when things get tough. Together, these two qualities form the backbone of long-term thriving. Thriving isn't about avoiding hardship - it's about developing the inner strength to push through it and come out stronger on the other side.

In this chapter, we'll explore what resilience and grit look like in practice, how to cultivate them in your life, and why they are essential to thriving in the long run.

What is Resilience?

Resilience is the psychological and emotional strength that helps you deal with stress, setbacks, and challenges. It's not about being invulnerable to pain or hardship - it's about being able to adapt, recover, and keep moving forward when life throws unexpected difficulties your way.

Resilience doesn't mean you won't feel stress, sadness, or frustration. Instead, it's about how quickly and effectively you can bounce back from those feelings and regain your balance. People who are resilient don't let challenges derail their progress. Instead, they use adversity as an opportunity to grow and learn.

A resilient mindset recognises that setbacks are temporary and that challenges are part of life. Rather than giving up or becoming overwhelmed, resilient people ask, "What can I learn from this? How can I use this experience to make myself stronger?"

Grit: The Long-Term Persistence to Succeed

While resilience helps you bounce back from short-term setbacks, grit is the quality that keeps you moving toward your long-term goals, even when progress feels slow or difficult. It's the perseverance to keep going when things don't go as planned.

Psychologist Angela Duckworth, who popularised the concept of grit in her book *Grit: The Power of Passion and Perseverance*, describes grit as the combination of passion and persistence over the long haul. According to Duckworth, grit is often a better predictor of success than talent or intelligence. It's the ability to stick with your goals, even when the going gets tough, and to keep pushing forward despite obstacles.

Serena Williams is a prime example of someone who embodies grit. Throughout her tennis career, Williams has faced numerous challenges, including injuries, setbacks, and intense competition. But her grit—her ability to stay committed to her goals and keep working hard, even when others might have given up - has allowed her to maintain her position as one of the greatest athletes of all time. It's not just her talent that's led to her success - it's her unwavering determination to keep improving, even in the face of adversity.

The Role of Failure in Building Resilience and Grit

Failure is an inevitable part of life, and it's also a critical component of building resilience and grit. No one achieves success without encountering setbacks along the way. The difference between those who thrive and those who don't is how they respond to failure.

Resilient people view failure not as a reflection of their worth but as a learning opportunity. Instead of being discouraged by mistakes or missteps, they use failure as feedback - a way to identify what went wrong and how they can improve. This mindset shift turns failure from something to be feared into something to be embraced.

Derren Brown, the famous illusionist and mentalist, is known for embracing failure as part of his learning process. In his early career, Brown often experienced moments where tricks went wrong, or performances didn't land as expected. But instead of being deterred by these failures, Brown used them as opportunities to refine his craft. He learned to view failure as an integral part of his growth, and this resilience allowed him to become one of the most innovative and successful performers in his field.

How to Cultivate Resilience and Grit

Resilience and grit aren't fixed traits - they are skills that can be developed over time. Here are practical ways to cultivate these qualities in your life:

1. Reframe Your Mindset Around Challenges

Instead of viewing challenges as insurmountable obstacles, start seeing them as opportunities for growth. When faced with a setback, ask yourself, "What can I learn from this?" By shifting your perspective, you can reduce the emotional impact of failure and turn adversity into a learning experience.

2. Develop a Strong Support System

Resilient people don't go through tough times alone. They rely on strong relationships with friends, family, or colleagues to provide emotional support and encouragement. Building a support system gives you a safety net to fall back on when things get difficult, helping you bounce back more quickly.

3. Practice Self-Compassion

One of the keys to resilience is self-compassion - the ability to be kind to yourself in moments of failure or difficulty. Instead of beating yourself up when things go wrong, practice talking to yourself with the same kindness and understanding you would offer a friend. This reduces the emotional toll of failure and helps you recover more quickly.

4. Break Down Long-Term Goals into Smaller Steps

Grit is all about long-term persistence, but that doesn't mean you need to tackle everything at once. Break your long-term goals into smaller, manageable steps. By focusing on incremental progress, you'll be less likely to feel overwhelmed, and each small victory will build your confidence and momentum.

5. Build Emotional Agility

Emotional agility is the ability to navigate your emotions without becoming overwhelmed by them. It involves recognising and naming your emotions without letting them dictate your behaviour. Practicing emotional agility allows you to stay resilient in the face of stress and setbacks because you're able to acknowledge your feelings without being controlled by them.

Practical Exercise: Building Resilience in Everyday Life

Building resilience and grit requires practice. Here's a simple exercise to help you start cultivating these qualities in your daily life:

1. **Identify a Recent Setback**: Think about a recent challenge or setback you've experienced. It could be something big, like a job loss, or something smaller, like a failed project at work.

2. **Reframe the Setback**: Write down how you initially felt about the setback. Then, rewrite your thoughts using a resilience mindset. For example, instead of thinking, "I failed," reframe it as, "This is a chance to learn and improve."

3. **Identify One Action to Move Forward**: What's one small action you can take to move forward from this setback? It could be seeking feedback, adjusting your approach, or simply taking time to reflect. The key is to focus on forward momentum, no matter how small the step.

4. **Practice Self-Compassion**: As you reflect on the setback, practice speaking to yourself with kindness. Acknowledge that setbacks are a normal part of life and that you're learning and growing through the process.

Lionel Richie: Resilience in Action

A powerful example of resilience in action is Lionel Richie's experience with the creation of the song *We Are the World*. When the project was first proposed, it seemed impossible to coordinate so many stars, manage their egos, and create something meaningful. But Richie's resilience and ability to navigate the emotional challenges of working with so many strong personalities helped bring the project to life.

Richie's resilience didn't just come from his ability to handle logistics - it came from his passion for the project's purpose and his unwavering belief that music could make a difference. His grit and determination ensured that *We Are the World* became one of the most iconic charity singles of all time, raising millions for humanitarian aid.

The Long-Term Benefits of Resilience and Grit

Developing resilience and grit has long-term benefits that go far beyond just achieving your goals. These qualities help you maintain your well-being, build stronger relationships, and approach life with a sense of optimism and hope, even in the face of difficulty.

When you cultivate resilience, you develop the ability to bounce back from adversity more quickly. Life's inevitable challenges no longer feel like insurmountable obstacles - they become opportunities to grow stronger and more capable. And with grit, you'll find that even the biggest challenges can be overcome with persistence and determination.

Key Takeaways:

- Resilience is the ability to bounce back from setbacks, while grit is the persistence to keep moving toward long-term goals.

- Failure is a necessary part of building resilience and grit. How you respond to failure determines your ability to thrive in the long run.

- Serena Williams, Derren Brown, and Lionel Richie exemplify resilience and grit through their persistence in the face of challenges.

- You can cultivate resilience and grit by reframing challenges, building a support system, practicing self-compassion, and breaking down long-term goals into manageable steps.

- Resilience and grit aren't just about achieving success—they're about thriving emotionally and mentally, no matter what life throws your way.

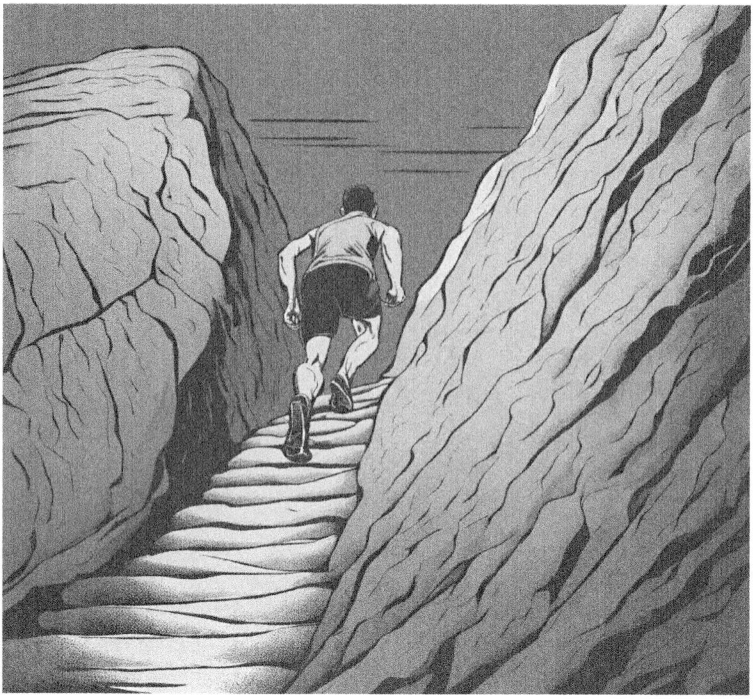

Chapter 7: Thriving in Uncertainty - Adapting to Change and Embracing the Unknown

Uncertainty is a constant in life. Whether it's economic shifts, technological advancements, or personal challenges, the world in 2025 is marked by rapid change and unpredictability. Yet, while uncertainty can feel unsettling, it also presents incredible opportunities for growth, innovation, and personal transformation.

Thriving in 2025 isn't about avoiding uncertainty - it's about learning to adapt, embrace the unknown, and stay resilient in the face of change. The key is to shift your mindset from fearing uncertainty to seeing it as an opportunity to evolve and discover new possibilities.

In this chapter, we'll explore how you can thrive in uncertain times by developing the skills and mindsets that enable you to adapt quickly, stay calm under pressure, and approach the unknown with curiosity and courage.

Why Uncertainty Feels So Uncomfortable

Humans are wired to seek stability and predictability. Our brains prefer to know what's coming next so we can plan and prepare. That's why uncertainty often triggers feelings of anxiety and discomfort - it disrupts the familiar and forces us into a space where the outcome is unknown.

But it's precisely in this space where the greatest opportunities for growth exist. When you step into the unknown, you're forced to think creatively, take risks, and discover new solutions. While uncertainty may feel uncomfortable, it's also the birthplace of innovation and personal development.

The key to thriving in uncertainty is not to eliminate it - because that's impossible - but to learn how to navigate it with confidence, flexibility, and resilience.

A Growth Mindset for Uncertainty

One of the most important shifts you can make to thrive in uncertainty is to adopt a growth mindset. As discussed earlier, a growth mindset is the belief that your abilities, intelligence, and skills can be developed through effort and learning. This mindset is particularly powerful when facing uncertain situations because it encourages you to view challenges as opportunities for growth rather than as threats.

With a growth mindset, you can approach uncertainty with curiosity instead of fear. You begin to ask yourself, "What can I learn from this situation?" or "How can I use this challenge to develop new skills?" This shift in thinking allows you to stay open to new possibilities, even when the outcome is unclear.

The Power of Adaptability

If there's one skill that will help you thrive in 2025, it's adaptability. Adaptability is the ability to adjust your thinking, behaviour, and strategies in response to changing circumstances. It's what enables you to stay flexible, pivot when needed, and find new ways to move forward when the original plan doesn't work out.

In uncertain times, being rigid or overly attached to specific outcomes can lead to frustration and burnout. But when you're adaptable, you're able to shift gears and find alternative solutions, even when things don't go as expected. Adaptability allows you to stay calm, focused, and resourceful in the face of change.

Chris Hadfield: Thriving in Space

A remarkable example of thriving in uncertainty comes from Chris Hadfield, the Canadian astronaut who became the first Canadian to command the International Space Station (ISS). As an astronaut, Hadfield lived and worked in one of the most unpredictable and high-stakes environments imaginable - space. From mechanical failures to health risks, astronauts face countless unknowns every day, and their ability to thrive depends on their adaptability, problem-solving skills, and emotional resilience.

Hadfield's time aboard the ISS required constant adaptability. When unexpected challenges arose - such as equipment malfunctions or health concerns - Hadfield and his team couldn't rely on immediate help. Instead, they had to think on their feet, work with limited resources, and stay calm under pressure.

Hadfield's approach to uncertainty was rooted in preparation, adaptability, and maintaining a positive mindset. He famously said, "There's no problem so bad that you can't make it worse," highlighting the importance of staying calm and measured in the face of challenges. His ability to embrace uncertainty allowed him to not only survive but thrive in the harshest and most unpredictable environment known to man.

Hadfield's experience shows that thriving in uncertainty is about being adaptable, staying calm under pressure, and finding solutions even when the odds are stacked against you.

Letting Go of Perfectionism

One of the biggest barriers to thriving in uncertainty is perfectionism. When we feel uncertain, our natural instinct is often to try to control every detail or outcome. But perfectionism can be paralysing, leading to procrastination, indecision, and unnecessary stress.

In uncertain situations, perfectionism is especially unhelpful because it prevents you from taking action. The fear of making mistakes or not getting things exactly right can stop you from moving forward, leaving you stuck in a cycle of overthinking.

To thrive in uncertainty, it's essential to let go of the need for perfection and embrace the idea that progress is better than perfection. The goal is not to avoid mistakes but to learn from them. By accepting that uncertainty inherently involves risk, and that mistakes are part of the process, you free yourself to take bold action and explore new possibilities.

Cliff Young: Thriving at Your Own Pace

A remarkable story of thriving in uncertainty comes from Cliff Young, the Australian potato farmer who became an unlikely champion in an ultra-marathon. In 1983, Young entered the Sydney to Melbourne ultra-marathon, a gruelling 544-mile race that typically attracted elite athletes. At 61 years old, Young showed up to the race in overalls and work boots, and most people didn't take him seriously.

But Young had a secret: while the other runners adhered to the conventional wisdom of running for 18 hours and then sleeping for six, Young adopted a different strategy. He didn't sleep. Instead, he shuffled along at his own pace throughout the entire race, covering ground steadily and consistently.

Despite the odds and the uncertainty of how his unorthodox method would fare, Young not only completed the race - he won it. His victory was a testament to the power of resilience, adaptability, and thriving in the face of uncertainty. Young wasn't the fastest, and he didn't have the most sophisticated training, but he succeeded by staying true to his own pace and embracing the unknown.

Strategies for Thriving in Uncertainty

Thriving in uncertainty isn't about having all the answers - it's about developing the mindset and strategies that allow you to navigate the unknown with confidence. Here are some practical ways to thrive in uncertain times:

1. Focus on What You Can Control

When faced with uncertainty, it's easy to get overwhelmed by everything that's outside of your control. But focusing on what you can control—your attitude, your actions, and your response to challenges—helps ground you in the present moment. Instead of worrying about what might happen, focus on the steps you can take right now to move forward.

2. Take Small, Consistent Actions

In uncertain situations, it's tempting to wait until you have all the information before making a decision. But waiting too long can lead to inaction. Instead, focus on taking small, consistent actions that move you in the direction of your goals. These actions don't have to be perfect—they just need to keep you moving forward.

3. Embrace Flexibility and Experimentation

Uncertainty often requires you to try new approaches and experiment with different strategies. Be willing to pivot when necessary and stay open to new possibilities. Flexibility is one of the most valuable qualities you can develop in uncertain times because it allows you to adapt and thrive, even when the original plan doesn't work out.

4. Cultivate Emotional Resilience

Emotional resilience is the ability to manage your emotions during stressful or uncertain situations. This involves recognising your feelings without letting them overwhelm you. Practicing mindfulness, meditation, or simply taking time to reflect on your emotions can help you stay centred and resilient in the face of uncertainty.

Practical Exercise: Adapting to Uncertainty

Here's an exercise to help you build your adaptability and resilience in uncertain situations:

1. **Identify an Area of Uncertainty**: Think about an area of your life where you're currently facing uncertainty. It could be a career decision, a personal challenge, or an unknown outcome.

2. **List What You Can Control**: Write down all the things you can control in this situation. Focus on your actions, mindset, and response to the uncertainty.

3. **Take One Small Action**: Choose one small action you can take today to move forward, even if it's just a tiny step. The goal is to create momentum, not to solve the entire problem in one go.

4. **Reflect on Your Emotions**: Take a moment to reflect on how this uncertainty is making you feel. Acknowledge your emotions without judgement, and remind yourself that it's okay to feel discomfort in the face of the unknown.

Key Takeaways:

- Uncertainty is a constant in life, but it's also an opportunity for growth, creativity, and innovation.

- Chris Hadfield demonstrates how adaptability and calmness in unpredictable situations are essential to thriving in challenging environments.

- Cliff Young's story shows that thriving in uncertainty sometimes means going at your own pace and finding unconventional solutions.

- Cultivate adaptability, flexibility, and emotional resilience to thrive in uncertain times.

- Let go of perfectionism and embrace small, consistent actions that create momentum in the face of the unknown.

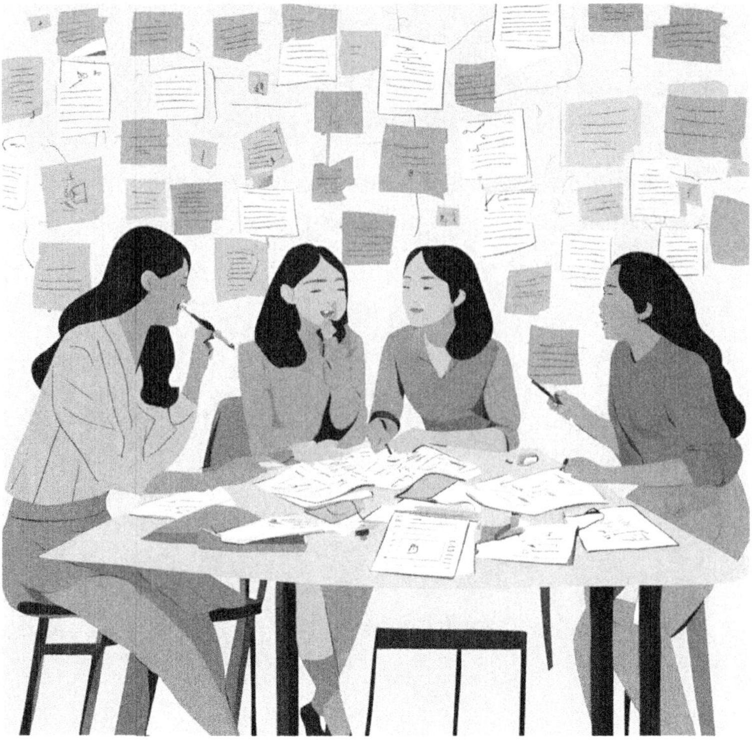

Chapter 8: Playfulness and Creativity - Thriving Through Innovation and Joy

When we think about thriving, we often focus on hard work, resilience, and determination. But thriving also requires something less obvious - playfulness and creativity. In a world that is constantly changing and often stressful, the ability to tap into your creative side, approach challenges with curiosity, and maintain a sense of joy can be one of the most powerful tools for thriving.

In 2025, creativity is not just for artists or entrepreneurs - it's for everyone. Whether you're navigating personal challenges, professional obstacles, or the unpredictable nature of life, creativity allows you to see new possibilities, solve problems in innovative ways, and stay adaptable in an ever-evolving world. And playfulness? It's the secret ingredient that keeps your spirit light and energised, even when things get tough.

In this chapter, we'll explore how embracing creativity, and playfulness can help you thrive, the science behind why these qualities are essential for well-being, and practical ways to bring more creativity and joy into your daily life.

The Power of Play

From the time we are children, play is a natural part of life. It's how we explore the world, learn new skills, and connect with others. But as we grow older, the concept of play often gets left behind, replaced by responsibilities, deadlines, and the pressure to be productive. However, research shows that play isn't just for kids - it's a crucial component of well-being for adults, too.

Play is about engaging in activities that are enjoyable, spontaneous, and free from the pressure to achieve a specific result. When you play, whether it's through games, hobbies, or creative pursuits, your brain shifts into a state of relaxation and openness. This not only reduces stress but also fosters creativity, problem-solving, and emotional resilience.

Keanu Reeves, known for his calm demeanour and versatility as an actor, is someone who brings playfulness to his career. Despite being known for action-packed roles in films like *The Matrix*, Reeves has always embraced a wide range of projects, from comedic roles to voice acting in animated films. His ability to stay open, experiment, and not take himself too seriously has allowed him to thrive in an industry known for its unpredictability. His playful approach to life and work is a reminder that embracing joy and curiosity is key to longevity and success.

Creativity as a Tool for Thriving

Creativity isn't limited to artistic endeavours - it's a mindset and a way of approaching challenges with curiosity and innovation. When you tap into your creativity, you're more likely to see possibilities that others overlook. Creativity helps you break free from rigid thinking, find new solutions, and adapt to changing circumstances.

Albert Einstein famously said, "Creativity is intelligence having fun." This quote captures the essence of why creativity is so powerful - it allows you to engage with the world in a way that's both thoughtful and playful. Creativity is not about being perfect or producing something "worthy" - it's about experimenting, making mistakes, and discovering new ways of thinking and doing.

In fact, research shows that when you're in a state of play or creativity, your brain enters a state known as "flow" - a mental state where you're fully immersed in an activity, lose track of time, and feel a deep sense of enjoyment. Flow not only boosts your well-being but also enhances your productivity and problem-solving abilities. The more you allow yourself to engage in creative activities, the more easily you'll find solutions to challenges, whether they're personal, professional, or emotional.

The Paperclip Experiment: The Creative Power of Playfulness

A fascinating study that demonstrates the power of creativity and playfulness is known as the paperclip experiment. In this experiment, participants are asked to come up with as many uses as possible for a simple paperclip. What the researchers found was that children consistently outperform adults in this task. Why? Because children approach the task with flexibility and imagination, unburdened by the "rules" that tend to limit adult thinking.

As we grow older, we become more rigid in our thinking, often adhering to the rules and frameworks we've learned over time. But thriving requires breaking out of these limitations and tapping into the playful, imaginative part of our brains. The paperclip experiment shows that creativity thrives when we're open to thinking outside the box, free from the constraints of how things "should" be done.

Incorporating playfulness into your problem-solving approach can lead to more innovative solutions. By giving yourself permission to think like a child again - without fear of judgment or failure - you unlock your full creative potential.

Dolly Parton: Playful and Creative in the Face of Challenges

Dolly Parton is a wonderful example of someone who embodies both playfulness and creativity in her career. While she is best known for her music, Parton has thrived in numerous creative ventures, from film to writing to her iconic theme park, Dollywood. What sets Parton apart is her ability to face challenges with a sense of humour and playfulness, while continuing to create, evolve, and inspire others.

When Parton first started her career, she faced resistance from the music industry because of her bold persona and unconventional style. But instead of conforming, she embraced her uniqueness, using humour and creativity to build a brand that has transcended generations. Parton's ability to be playful and creative, even in the face of adversity, has been a key factor in her long-lasting success.

Her approach shows us that playfulness isn't frivolous - it's a powerful tool for resilience. It helps you stay light-hearted in the face of challenges, take risks without fear of failure, and continue creating in the face of uncertainty.

How to Cultivate Playfulness and Creativity in Your Life

You don't have to be an artist or a performer to bring more creativity and playfulness into your life. These qualities are accessible to everyone and can be integrated into your daily routine in simple yet meaningful ways. Here are some strategies to help you tap into your creative and playful side:

1. Make Time for Play

Just as you schedule work tasks or meetings, make time in your day for play. This could be anything that brings you joy - whether it's playing a game, engaging in a hobby, or simply doing something fun with friends or family. The key is to give yourself permission to engage in activities that have no agenda other than to enjoy yourself.

2. Practice Creative Problem-Solving

The next time you're faced with a challenge, approach it from a creative mindset. Instead of immediately trying to solve the problem in a conventional way, ask yourself, "What are some unusual or playful solutions to this?" Give yourself the freedom to brainstorm without judgment, even if the ideas seem outlandish at first. Creativity often flourishes when you allow yourself to explore unconventional possibilities.

3. Embrace Mistakes

Part of what makes play and creativity so powerful is that they encourage experimentation. Mistakes aren't failures - they're opportunities to learn and grow. Whether you're learning a new skill, trying a creative project, or solving a problem, embrace the possibility of making mistakes along the way. The more you allow yourself to experiment without fear of failure, the more creative and resilient you'll become.

4. Surround Yourself with Inspiration

Creativity thrives in environments that are stimulating and inspiring. Surround yourself with things that spark your imagination - whether it's art, books, music, or nature. The more you immerse yourself in creativity, the more likely you are to feel inspired and motivated to bring that energy into your own life.

Practical Exercise: Cultivating Playfulness and Creativity

Here's a fun exercise to help you tap into your creative side and incorporate playfulness into your daily routine:

1. **Try a New Hobby**: Pick a hobby or activity you've never tried before, something that piques your interest but doesn't come with any pressure to excel. Whether it's painting, dancing, playing an instrument, or trying a new sport, the goal is to engage in an activity purely for fun.

2. **Brainstorm Playfully**: Choose a problem you're currently facing in your personal or professional life. Set a timer for 10 minutes and brainstorm as many playful, out-of-the-box solutions as you can. Don't worry about whether the ideas are "good" or "realistic" - just let your imagination run wild.

3. **Schedule a Play Date**: Block out time in your schedule for a "play date" with yourself or with friends. This could involve anything from playing a board game to going to an escape room or having a creative brainstorming session. The point is to make time for fun and creativity without any expectations or goals.

James Blunt: Playfulness in the Face of Criticism

James Blunt, after achieving massive success with his hit song *You're Beautiful*, faced a wave of public backlash, particularly on social media. Instead of retreating or responding defensively, Blunt took a playful approach. He responded to the criticism with witty, sarcastic, and often self-deprecating humour, turning the situation on its head.

Blunt's ability to remain playful and not take himself too seriously allowed him to maintain his sense of joy and connection with his audience, despite the negativity. His response to criticism shows that playfulness isn't just about having fun - it's a way to defuse tension, build resilience, and continue thriving even in challenging situations.

Key Takeaways:

- Playfulness and creativity are essential qualities for thriving in 2025. They help reduce stress, foster innovation, and keep you adaptable in the face of challenges.

- Keanu Reeves and Dolly Parton demonstrate how playfulness and creativity can lead to lasting success by staying open to new opportunities and embracing joy in their work.

- The paperclip experiment shows that children outperform adults in creative tasks because they approach problems with playfulness and flexibility.

- Incorporating play and creativity into your daily life can be as simple as trying new hobbies, brainstorming creatively, and allowing yourself to make mistakes.

- James Blunt's playful responses to public criticism are a powerful example of how humour and light-heartedness can help you navigate adversity and continue thriving.

How am I Thriving? - Midpoint Review

Congratulations, you're now halfway through your book!

I hope you're finding the book not just interesting, but more importantly, useful! Here are a few questions to reflect on your progress so far.

- What have you learned from this book so far?
- What key concepts or ideas do you remember?
- What have you changed in your life?
- What have you intended to change but still not yet taken any action? Why? (be honest!)
- What's on your list to do next?
- How are you currently thriving?

Use this space below to make a few notes based on your answers.

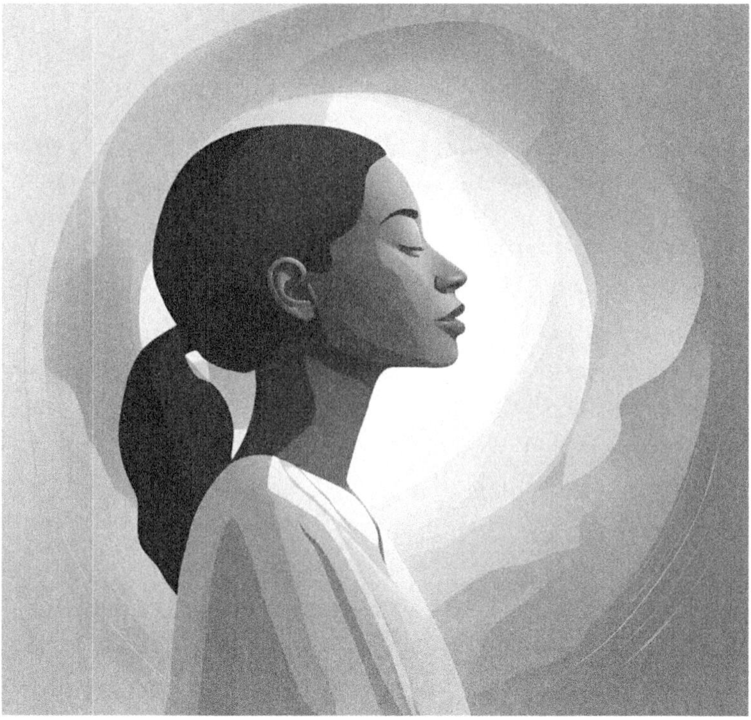

Chapter 9: The Power of Emotional Intelligence - Cultivating Self-Awareness and Empathy

Thriving isn't just about achieving personal success - it's also about building strong, fulfilling relationships with the people around you. In 2025, emotional intelligence (EI) will be more important than ever. As technology advances and workplaces become more dynamic, emotional intelligence will set apart those who can thrive in their interactions with others.

Emotional intelligence is the ability to recognise, understand, and manage your own emotions, as well as the emotions of others. It plays a crucial role in fostering healthy relationships, resolving conflicts, and building trust. Emotional intelligence isn't just about being empathetic - it's about being aware of how emotions influence behaviour and knowing how to navigate those emotions to create positive outcomes in your interactions.

In this chapter, we'll explore how emotional intelligence helps you thrive in relationships, why it's critical to long-term success, how you can develop your EI, and how to incorporate tools like anchoring from NLP (Neuro Linguistic Programming) to manage emotions effectively.

What is Emotional Intelligence?

Emotional intelligence involves several key skills that help you manage your emotions and relationships effectively. These include:

1. **Self-awareness**: The ability to recognise and understand your own emotions and how they affect your thoughts and actions.

2. **Self-management**: The ability to control impulsive feelings and behaviours, manage your emotions in healthy ways, and take initiative.

3. **Empathy**: The ability to understand and share the feelings of others, recognising their emotional needs and responding accordingly.

4. **Social skills**: The ability to manage relationships, build connections, and navigate social dynamics effectively.

Together, these skills form the foundation of emotional intelligence and are essential for building meaningful relationships, both in your personal life and in the workplace.

1. Practice Self-Awareness

Self-awareness is the foundation of emotional intelligence. It's the ability to understand your own emotions and how they impact your thoughts, behaviours, and interactions with others. The more you understand your emotions, the better equipped you are to manage them, make thoughtful decisions, and respond to others in a balanced way.

To practice self-awareness, it's important to regularly check in with yourself and ask, "How am I feeling?" This simple question helps you take a pause and reflect on your emotional state. When you're in touch with your emotions, you're more likely to respond thoughtfully, rather than reacting impulsively. Taking the time to be aware of your feelings is the first step toward managing them effectively.

Practical Tip: Daily Reflection for Self-Awareness

Set aside time each day to reflect on your emotional state. Ask yourself, "How am I feeling right now?" and give yourself space to fully recognise and understand those feelings. Regularly checking in with yourself helps you stay attuned to your emotions and ensures you're not ignoring or suppressing how you feel.

2. Develop Self-Management Skills

Self-management is all about controlling your impulses and staying focused, even when emotions run high. It's the ability to keep your emotions in check and make thoughtful decisions, rather than reacting impulsively. People who excel at self-management can navigate stressful or emotionally charged situations without being overwhelmed by their emotions.

For example, imagine you're in a meeting and a colleague criticises your work in front of others. The initial emotional response might be anger or embarrassment, leading to a defensive reaction. But with strong self-management skills, you can take a moment to pause, recognise your emotional response, and choose a more measured, constructive reaction.

Practical Tip: The Power of the Pause

The next time you feel overwhelmed by emotions, practice taking a pause. Deep breathing is a simple but effective way to calm your nervous system and give yourself space to think. Count to ten, take a few slow, deep breaths, or step away from the situation for a moment. This pause will give you time to process your emotions and respond with clarity, rather than reacting impulsively.

3. Cultivate Empathy

Empathy is the ability to understand and share the feelings of others. It's one of the most important components of emotional intelligence because it allows you to connect with people on a deeper level and build trust. Empathy helps you navigate difficult conversations, resolve conflicts, and foster strong relationships.

Oprah Winfrey, known for her remarkable emotional intelligence, built her media empire not just on her business acumen but also on her deep empathy for others. Whether interviewing guests or leading philanthropic efforts, Oprah's ability to understand and validate the emotions of those around her has been central to her success. Her empathy has enabled her to connect with audiences globally and build lasting relationships with people from all walks of life.

Empathy doesn't mean you have to agree with someone's perspective, but it does mean you're able to see the situation from their point of view. This skill is critical for effective communication and conflict resolution.

Practical Tip: Practice Active Listening

When you're in a conversation, focus on truly understanding the other person's emotions, rather than just waiting for your turn to speak. Ask open-ended questions like, "How are you feeling about that?" or "What's been on your mind lately?" Active listening helps you pick up on emotional cues and respond with empathy, deepening your connections with others.

---

4. Improve Your Social Skills

Strong social skills are key to relationship management. Emotional intelligence helps you navigate social dynamics, manage conflicts, and build positive relationships in both personal and professional settings. People with strong social skills are able to communicate effectively, collaborate with others, and resolve disputes without escalating tensions.

Effective social skills also involve the ability to build rapport with others, create positive interactions, and maintain harmonious relationships, even in challenging situations. In the workplace, strong social skills are essential for leadership, teamwork, and building a positive organisational culture.

Satya Nadella, the CEO of Microsoft, is a great example of someone who has demonstrated exceptional emotional intelligence in leadership. When Nadella took over as CEO, he focused on creating a culture of empathy and collaboration, encouraging open communication and emotional awareness within the company. Under his leadership, Microsoft has experienced significant growth, not just in terms of profits but also in terms of workplace culture and employee satisfaction.

Nadella's focus on empathy, emotional intelligence, and relationship-building has transformed Microsoft's culture, proving that thriving in business requires more than just technical expertise - it requires the ability to connect with people on a human level.

Practical Tip: Build Rapport and Communicate Clearly

Focus on building rapport with others by finding common ground and showing genuine interest in their lives. Practice clear communication by being mindful of your tone, body language, and the emotions of those around you. Express gratitude and appreciation regularly and take the time to acknowledge the contributions of others.

Anchoring: Using NLP to Manage Emotions

One of the most powerful techniques for managing emotions is anchoring, a tool from Neuro-Linguistic Programming (NLP) that allows you to create positive emotional states on demand. Anchoring helps you access feelings of confidence, calmness, or motivation by associating those emotions with a specific trigger, such as a word, gesture, or action.

Here's a breakdown of how anchoring works:

1. **Identify a Desired State**: The first step is to identify the positive emotional state you want to anchor, such as confidence, calmness, motivation, or happiness. You might recall a time when you felt that way or imagine what it would feel like.

2. **Choose a Trigger**: Select a unique trigger to associate with the positive state. It could be a physical action (e.g., touching your thumb and forefinger together), a word or phrase (e.g., "I've got this"), or a specific visual or auditory cue. The trigger should be something that can easily be replicated and isn't overly common, so it maintains its effectiveness.

3. **Experience the State Fully**: To set the anchor, immerse yourself in the positive state. Use visualisation techniques, recall vivid memories, and focus on the emotions and sensations in your body. The more intense the experience, the stronger the anchor will be.

4. **Anchor the Trigger**: While fully experiencing the positive state, activate your chosen trigger. For example, if it's a physical action like pressing your thumb and forefinger together, do this at the peak of the emotional experience. This connection between the action and the state forms the anchor.

5. **Repeat and Reinforce**: The more you practice this, the stronger the anchor becomes. Repeat the process several times to ensure the trigger is deeply associated with the positive state.

6. **Use the Trigger When Needed**: Once the anchor is established, you can use it to quickly access the positive emotional state whenever you need it. For example, before a public speaking event, you might activate your trigger to feel confident and calm.

Practical Exercise: Try Anchoring

1. **Choose a Positive State**: Think of a time when you felt confident or calm. Relive the experience vividly.

2. **Set Your Trigger**: As you experience the positive state, choose your trigger, such as pressing your thumb and forefinger together.

3. **Activate Your Anchor**: Use the trigger to anchor the positive emotion and repeat the process to strengthen the connection.

4. **Test It**: When you need a boost of confidence or calmness, use the anchor and notice how it helps you shift into that state.

Key Takeaways:

- Emotional intelligence is essential for thriving in relationships, both personal and professional.
- Self-awareness helps you understand and manage your emotions, leading to more thoughtful actions.
- Self-management allows you to control impulsive reactions and stay calm under pressure.
- Empathy fosters deeper connections and helps you navigate difficult conversations.
- Strong social skills are key to building positive relationships and resolving conflicts.
- Anchoring is a powerful tool from NLP that allows you to access positive emotional states by associating them with specific triggers.

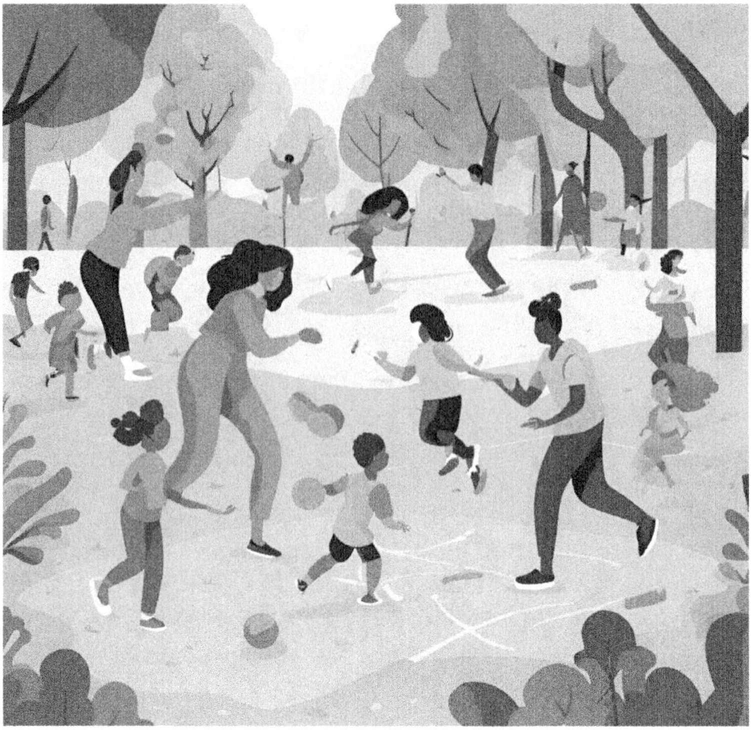

Chapter 10: The Joy of Play - Building Resilience Through Fun and Experimentation

In the hustle and bustle of life, we often associate thriving with hard work, productivity, and achieving goals. While these are crucial components, there's another vital ingredient that many of us overlook - playfulness. As adults, we tend to view play as something only children indulge in, but the truth is that play is essential for our well-being, creativity, and resilience. It's through play that we can learn to adapt, recharge, and face life's challenges with a lighter heart and clearer mind.

Play isn't frivolous or a waste of time. It's a powerful way to build mental and emotional strength. By engaging in activities that bring joy, spark curiosity, and let you experiment without fear of failure, you not only refresh your mind but also boost your resilience.

In this chapter, we'll explore how tapping into the joy of play can help you thrive, why it's essential to experiment and take risks, and practical ways to incorporate more playfulness into your daily routine.

The Importance of Play in Adulthood

Play is often seen as a luxury in adulthood, something we feel guilty about because it doesn't seem "productive." But play is not just about taking a break - it's about nourishing your mind, body, and soul. Whether you're engaging in physical play like sports or mental play like solving puzzles, play creates a sense of flow, where you're fully immersed in the moment.

The idea of play goes beyond just having fun; it enhances your ability to adapt to changing circumstances and build resilience in the face of stress. When you're in a playful mindset, you're more likely to be open to new ideas, think creatively, and bounce back from setbacks. This openness is crucial for thriving in a world that is constantly evolving.

The Science Behind Play and Resilience

Play has been shown to activate the reward centres of the brain, releasing dopamine and endorphins, which boost mood and reduce stress. It also fosters neuroplasticity, the brain's ability to form new connections and adapt to new experiences. This makes play essential not just for relaxation but for cognitive growth and emotional resilience.

Research in positive psychology shows that play helps individuals handle adversity more effectively. It promotes a growth mindset, allowing you to view challenges as opportunities for learning and experimentation, rather than threats. This mindset is key to thriving, as it helps you remain flexible and optimistic in the face of difficulties.

Why Experimentation is Vital for Growth

Playfulness is closely linked to the idea of experimentation - the willingness to try new things without the fear of failure. When you experiment, you're open to making mistakes, learning from them, and finding new pathways to success. This mindset is crucial in a rapidly changing world where uncertainty is the norm.

James Blunt provides a great example of someone who used playfulness and experimentation to navigate public criticism. After his hit song *You're Beautiful* became overplayed, he faced a wave of backlash, especially on social media. Instead of taking the criticism to heart, Blunt used humour and playful, witty responses to defuse the negativity. His ability to turn criticism into playful banter not only helped him maintain his public image but also deepened his connection with fans.

Blunt's approach reminds us that when you don't take yourself too seriously, you can weather criticism, mistakes, and setbacks with resilience. Playfulness allows you to experiment with different responses and ultimately thrive in challenging situations.

Practical Ways to Incorporate Play and Experimentation into Your Life

The benefits of play and experimentation are clear, but how do you bring more of it into your daily life? Here are some practical ways to cultivate playfulness and build resilience through fun and experimentation:

1. Try Something New Without the Pressure to Succeed

Pick an activity or hobby that you've never tried before but let go of the pressure to be good at it. Whether it's painting, dancing, or learning a new language, the goal is to engage with something new purely for the sake of exploration and enjoyment. Allowing yourself to be a beginner fosters humility and keeps your mind open to new possibilities.

2. Create a 'Playtime' in Your Day

Set aside dedicated time each day or week for play. This could be anything from playing a board game with friends, going for a hike, or building something with your hands. Make this a regular part of your routine, not as a luxury, but as an essential activity for your well-being.

3. Embrace Mistakes as Part of the Process

Mistakes are an inevitable part of learning and growth. Embrace them as opportunities to learn, rather than reasons to give up. Experiment with new ways of doing things, and don't be afraid to fail. When you approach challenges with a playful mindset, you're more likely to find creative solutions and build resilience.

4. Engage in Group Play

Playing with others - whether it's through team sports, group games, or collaborative creative projects - can strengthen social bonds and create a sense of shared joy. Group play encourages cooperation, fosters connection, and builds emotional resilience as you support one another through the ups and downs of the activity.

Dolly Parton: Playfulness as a Tool for Success

Dolly Parton, often seen as a playful and joyful figure, is a shining example of someone who has thrived by embracing fun and creativity throughout her career. Despite facing countless challenges and industry expectations, she's managed to keep her sense of humour and playfulness at the forefront of everything she does. From her iconic songs to her bold persona, Parton shows that thriving is not just about hard work - it's about infusing joy and playfulness into the process.

Her playfulness has allowed her to take risks, push boundaries, and experiment with new ventures, from music to acting to creating her theme park, Dollywood. Parton's ability to approach her work with light-heartedness and a willingness to try new things is a key factor in her long-lasting success.

Practical Exercise: Play Your Way to Resilience

Here's an exercise to help you incorporate more play and experimentation into your life:

1. **Identify an Area of Your Life that Feels Stuck**: Think about an area of your life where you feel stuck or uninspired. It could be work-related, a personal project, or even your social life.

2. **Approach it Playfully**: Instead of focusing on how to solve the problem or achieve a particular outcome, brainstorm playful, creative ways to approach it. Ask yourself, "How can I make this fun?" or "What would happen if I experimented with a new way of doing this?"

3. **Take One Playful Action**: Choose one of your ideas and try it out, without worrying about whether it will work. Focus on the process of experimenting, learning, and enjoying the experience.

4. **Reflect on the Outcome**: After trying your playful approach, reflect on what you learned. Did you discover something new about the situation? Did it shift your mindset? How can you continue to incorporate more play into this area of your life?

Key Takeaways:

- Playfulness is a vital tool for thriving, not just for relaxation but for building resilience, creativity, and joy.

- Experimentation allows you to take risks and learn from mistakes, fostering growth and adaptability.

- James Blunt and Dolly Parton exemplify how playful experimentation can turn challenges into opportunities for connection and success.

- Incorporating play and fun into your daily life can help you thrive emotionally and mentally, giving you the resilience to face challenges with optimism and creativity.

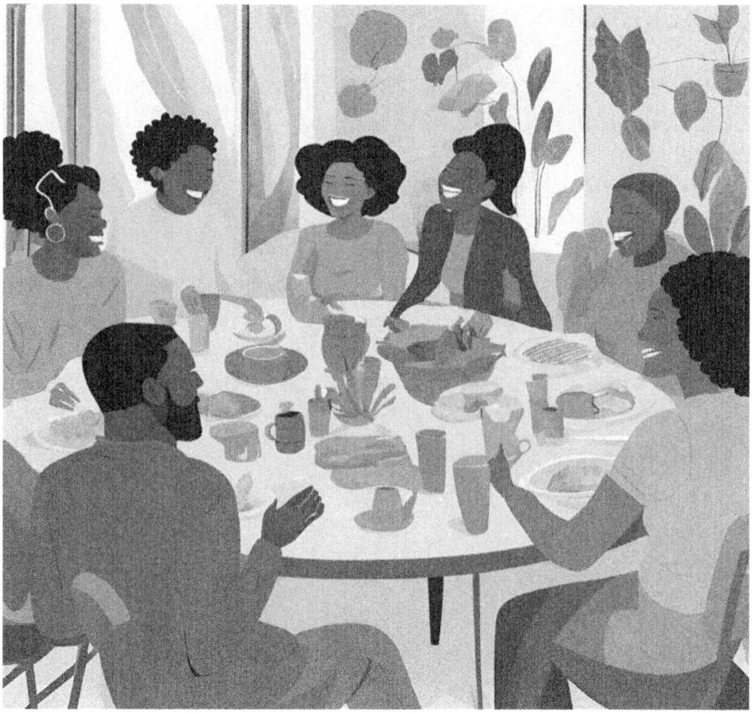

Chapter 11: Connection and Community - Thriving Together, Not Alone

Humans are inherently social creatures. Even in an age where technology connects us more than ever, true connection and a sense of community remain essential for our well-being. Thriving isn't something that happens in isolation - it happens when we are part of something bigger than ourselves, whether it's through family, friends, work, or community groups.

In 2025, with technology rapidly changing the way we interact, the ability to build meaningful connections and contribute to a community will be critical to thriving. It's through these relationships that we find support, purpose, and a sense of belonging.

In this chapter, we'll explore how connection and community are foundational to thriving, why they matter more than ever, and practical ways to foster deeper relationships and build a thriving community around you.

The Importance of Connection for Well-being

Social connection is one of the most important predictors of happiness and well-being. Research consistently shows that people with strong social connections have lower levels of anxiety and depression, better physical health, and higher levels of emotional resilience. Having a support network helps you manage stress, provides a sense of belonging, and gives you the emotional tools to handle life's ups and downs.

In contrast, isolation and loneliness can have devastating effects on both mental and physical health. Studies have shown that chronic loneliness is as harmful to your health as smoking or obesity. This is why building and maintaining meaningful connections is so vital to thriving.

Connection is not just about being surrounded by people - it's about feeling understood, valued, and supported by others. True connection comes from deep, meaningful relationships where you can be yourself and feel a genuine sense of belonging.

Community as a Source of Strength

While individual connections are important, being part of a community offers a different kind of strength. Community provides a sense of shared purpose and a feeling of being part of something greater than yourself. Whether it's through work, hobbies, or shared values, communities can offer emotional support, collaboration, and opportunities for growth.

Mike Rosenberg, the singer-songwriter from Passenger, offers a powerful example of the role of community in thriving. Before rising to fame, Mike spent years busking on the streets, connecting with people through his music in a very personal and raw way. Even after achieving global success, he never forgot the importance of community and connection.

During the COVID-19 pandemic, when many people were struggling with isolation and uncertainty, Mike respected the challenges people faced and responded by hosting online concerts, bringing music and a sense of togetherness to fans around the world. His willingness to stay connected to his community, even in times of adversity, is a testament to how much we need human connection to thrive.

Mike's story illustrates how communities, whether physical or virtual, can provide support, uplift each other, and create a sense of shared purpose, even in difficult times. Thanks Mike, I'm a big fan of your music!

Why Building Deep Connections Can Be Challenging

In today's fast-paced, technology-driven world, building deep, meaningful connections can feel more challenging than ever. With social media and instant messaging, we are constantly connected, yet many people feel more isolated than ever. Part of the challenge comes from the tendency to form shallow, surface-level relationships that don't provide the depth or support needed for true connection.

True connection requires vulnerability, time, and effort. It means being open to others, sharing your authentic self, and investing in the relationships that matter. It also involves understanding that connection is a two-way street - giving support is just as important as receiving it.

Practical Ways to Build Connection and Community

Building stronger connections and fostering a sense of community doesn't have to be complicated. Here are some practical steps you can take to deepen your relationships and cultivate a thriving community around you:

1. Invest Time in Your Relationships

Make time for the people who matter to you. Whether it's through regular meetups, phone calls, or even video chats, consistently showing up for others helps strengthen your bonds. Deep relationships don't just happen - they require attention and care.

2. Be Present and Practice Active Listening

When you're with others, practice being fully present. Avoid distractions like checking your phone or thinking about your to-do list. Instead, focus on listening actively to what the other person is saying. Ask thoughtful questions, show empathy, and offer support when needed.

3. Find Your Tribe

Whether it's through shared hobbies, interests, or values, finding a group of people who understand and support you can make a huge difference in your well-being. Look for opportunities to join or create communities that align with your passions, whether it's a book club, a fitness group, or a professional network.

4. Give Back to Your Community

Thriving isn't just about what you get from others - it's about what you give. Volunteering, mentoring, or contributing your skills to a cause you care about can provide a sense of purpose and strengthen your ties to your community. The act of giving back often fosters deeper connections and creates a sense of fulfilment.

Lionel Richie: Community as a Driving Force

Another powerful example of community driving success comes from Lionel Richie and his experience with the global hit *We Are the World*. Richie's ability to bring together a diverse group of musicians for a single cause is a shining example of how collaboration and community can create something much greater than the sum of its parts.

When Richie co-wrote and produced *We Are the World*, he brought together some of the biggest stars in the music industry to raise money for humanitarian aid in Africa. The success of the song wasn't just about individual talent—it was about the power of a collective vision. Richie understood that thriving in a community requires bringing people together for a shared purpose and leveraging everyone's unique contributions.

Richie's story shows that thriving in a community isn't about competing with others—it's about working together, supporting one another, and striving toward a common goal.

The Digital Age: Connecting Virtually, but Meaningfully

As technology advances, many of our communities are now virtual. While face-to-face connection is invaluable, online communities can also offer support and a sense of belonging, especially in times when physical connection isn't possible. The key to thriving in digital communities is to seek depth in your interactions rather than just quantity.

Be intentional about your online connections - join groups or platforms that align with your values and interests. Take time to engage in meaningful conversations, offer support, and build genuine relationships online. Virtual connection, when approached thoughtfully, can be just as enriching as in-person interactions.

Practical Exercise: Strengthening Your Community Connections

Here's an exercise to help you focus on building deeper connections and fostering a thriving community:

1. **Identify Key Relationships**: Think about the most important relationships in your life, whether they are personal, professional, or within your community.

2. **Reach Out**: Make a point to reach out to someone you care about but haven't connected with in a while. It could be a friend, a family member, or a colleague. Take the time to listen to what's going on in their life and offer your support.

3. **Join or Re-engage with a Community**: If you've drifted away from a community you used to be part of, consider re-engaging. Or seek out a new community that aligns with your interests or goals.

4. **Give Back**: Look for a way to contribute to your community, whether it's through volunteering, mentoring, or simply offering your time and skills. Helping others strengthens your sense of connection and purpose.

Key Takeaways:

- Thriving requires connection and community—humans are wired for social bonds and thrive when they feel supported.

- Building meaningful relationships takes time, effort, and vulnerability, but it is essential for emotional well-being and resilience.

- Mike Rosenberg (Passenger) and Lionel Richie show how fostering community through music and collaboration can create something bigger than oneself.

- Whether through face-to-face interaction or online communities, investing in relationships and contributing to a shared purpose helps build resilience and long-term fulfilment.

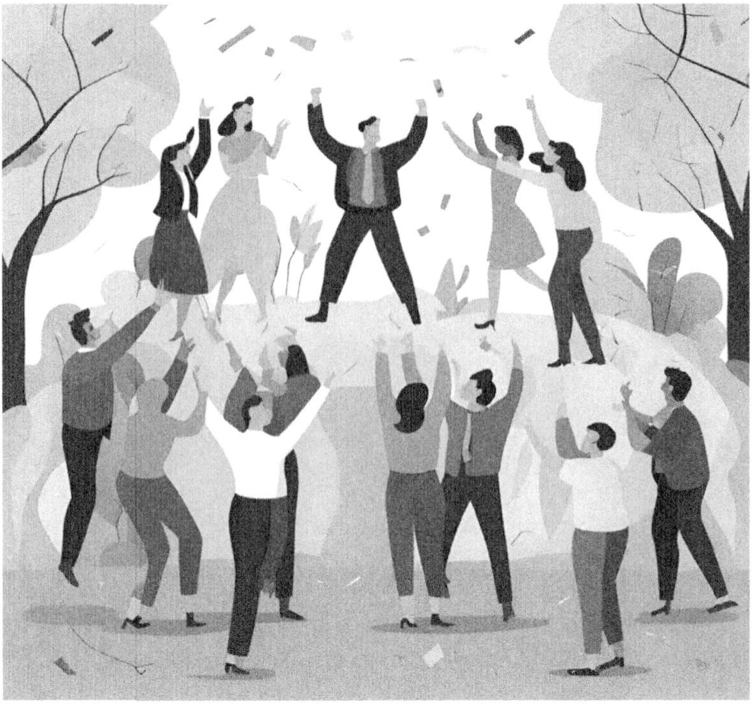

Chapter 12: Redefining Success - Beyond Traditional Measures

In a world that's constantly changing, the traditional definitions of success - wealth, status, and power - are beginning to feel outdated for many. While these markers can be important, they no longer encompass the full scope of what it means to thrive. In 2025, success is about more than climbing the corporate ladder or acquiring material possessions; it's about finding fulfilment, joy, and purpose in both your personal and professional life.

The shift in how we define success is profound, and it requires a change in mindset. For many, thriving means moving beyond the external measures of success society often celebrates and embracing a more personal, holistic view. Success becomes about aligning with your values, fostering meaningful relationships, and making a positive impact, rather than merely achieving titles, wealth, or recognition.

In this chapter, we'll explore how to redefine success in a way that aligns with your true self, why it's essential for thriving, and how to avoid the traps of chasing superficial goals.

Traditional Success: Why It's Often Not Enough

For much of history, success has been defined by external markers - how much money you make, what title you hold, how many accolades you've accumulated. While these traditional measures can be important, they often leave people feeling unfulfilled or disconnected from their true purpose. Chasing these external forms of success can lead to burnout, dissatisfaction, and a sense that no matter how much you achieve, it's never enough.

Many high achievers reach a point where they've "made it" by society's standards, yet still feel something is missing. They might have a successful career, a nice home, and financial security, but without a deeper sense of purpose or joy, these achievements can feel hollow. This disconnect between external success and internal fulfilment is one of the reasons why it's so important to redefine success on your own terms.

Dolly Parton: Success by Being Authentic

Few people exemplify the power of redefining success as well as Dolly Parton. While she's undoubtedly achieved immense success by traditional measures - countless hit songs, awards, and a thriving entertainment empire - what truly sets her apart is her commitment to staying true to herself. Parton has always embraced her unique style, personality, and values, even when the entertainment industry tried to push her in different directions.

In an industry that often prioritizes conformity, Dolly Parton built her success on authenticity. She didn't change herself to fit the mold of what a female country singer "should" look or sound like. Instead, she leaned into her individuality, humour, and resilience. This authenticity has made her not only a musical icon but also a beloved figure across generations.

For Parton, success has never been just about money or fame. It's been about making a positive impact, staying true to her roots, and giving back to others. Through her Imagination Library - a program that provides free books to children - Parton has demonstrated that success is as much about creating lasting, meaningful contributions as it is about personal achievement.

Parton's story reminds us that true success comes from living in alignment with your values and embracing your authentic self, rather than chasing societal expectations.

Redefining Success in the Digital Age

The rise of social media and digital culture has added another layer of complexity to how we view success. In today's world, success is often equated with visibility - the number of followers you have, the likes you receive, or the status of your online presence. The pressure to curate a perfect life online can lead to unrealistic expectations and a distorted sense of what it means to be successful.

Many people feel compelled to pursue external validation through social media, constantly comparing their lives to others and measuring their worth based on likes, shares, or followers. However, these metrics of success are often superficial and don't reflect the true value of one's life or contributions.

Cal Newport, author of *Digital Minimalism* and *Deep Work*, advocates for stepping back from the constant need for digital validation and focusing on meaningful accomplishments. Newport argues that real success is found in the depth of your work, your relationships, and your personal growth - not in how many people "like" your photos or follow you online.

Newport's message is clear: while technology can be a powerful tool for growth and connection, it shouldn't define our success. Thriving in the digital age requires reclaiming your time, attention, and energy to focus on what truly matters, rather than getting lost in the noise of online metrics.

The Role of Purpose in Redefining Success

At the heart of redefining success is the concept of purpose. Success, when redefined, is often less about what you achieve and more about why you achieve it. Purpose gives meaning to your accomplishments, making them feel worthwhile even if they don't lead to traditional forms of recognition.

Howard Schultz, the former CEO of Starbucks, built his entire company around the idea of purpose. While Starbucks is undoubtedly a commercial success, Schultz always emphasized that the company's true mission was to create a sense of community and connection. Schultz's vision was about more than just selling coffee; it was about creating a "third place" where people could feel a sense of belonging.

Schultz's commitment to purpose helped Starbucks thrive, but it also allowed him to redefine success for himself and his company. By focusing on impact and connection, Schultz showed that businesses can succeed not just by turning a profit, but by making a positive difference in the lives of customers and employees.

When you define success through the lens of purpose, it becomes less about hitting specific external targets and more about whether you are living in alignment with your values. Purpose-driven success is sustainable because it taps into something deeper than fleeting accomplishments.

Lionel Richie and the Power of Collective Success

Success isn't always an individual journey. Sometimes, it's about creating something meaningful through collaboration. Lionel Richie's experience with *We Are the World* is a perfect example of how collective success can be far more impactful than individual achievement.

When Richie co-wrote and produced *We Are the World*, he brought together a diverse group of the world's biggest musical talents to raise money for famine relief in Africa. The success of the song wasn't just measured by its commercial success - it became an anthem of global unity and purpose. Richie understood that thriving sometimes means working together toward a common goal and that collective success can have a lasting impact.

The story of *We Are the World* reminds us that success doesn't have to be about standing out as an individual. Sometimes, true success comes from working with others, contributing your unique talents to a shared vision, and making a positive difference in the world.

The Pitfalls of Chasing External Success

One of the biggest traps in the pursuit of success is the tendency to chase external markers without considering your internal fulfilment. This often leads to a cycle of overwork, burnout, and a constant feeling that you're not doing enough, no matter how much you achieve.

In many industries, especially in corporate environments, there's an unspoken pressure to constantly push for more - more hours, more output, more recognition. This can create a culture of overwork where success is defined by how much you sacrifice for your job, rather than by the quality of your life.

Thriving isn't about putting up with overwork, unrealistic deadlines, working weekends, or tolerating poor leadership. It's about creating boundaries, finding balance, and ensuring that your definition of success includes your health, relationships, and personal well-being.

It's important to recognize that success should never come at the expense of your mental or physical health. True success means taking care of yourself while achieving your goals, not sacrificing your well-being in the process.

Practical Steps to Redefine Success

Redefining success is a personal journey, but there are practical steps you can take to ensure your definition aligns with your true self:

1. Reflect on Your Values

Take time to reflect on what truly matters to you. What are your core values? What brings you joy, fulfilment, and a sense of purpose? Write down your values and use them as a guide when setting goals or making decisions about your career and life.

2. Focus on Impact, Not Status

Shift your focus from how much recognition you receive to the impact you're making. Whether it's in your job, your community, or your relationships, success should be measured by the positive difference you're making, not by the titles or accolades you earn.

3. Set Boundaries

Protect your well-being by setting clear boundaries around your work and personal life. Success should include time for rest, connection, and self-care. Don't fall into the trap of thinking that success means constantly working or being available 24/7.

4. Embrace Collaboration

Consider how you can collaborate with others to achieve success that's more impactful than individual accomplishment. Working with others can open doors to new opportunities, broaden your perspective, and create shared success.

Practical Exercise: Redefining Your Own Success

Here's an exercise to help you redefine success in a way that aligns with your personal values:

1. **List Your Achievements**: Write down some of your recent achievements, both personal and professional. Don't just focus on the big accomplishments—include the small wins as well. Here are a few of my small wins that I've appreciated whilst writing this book:

    1. Writing the 1st draft of this book!
    2. Selling my classic car
    3. Getting to see friends more
    4. Unsubscribing from advertising emails
    5. Learning how to use ai

2. **Reflect on Their Meaning**: For each achievement, ask yourself, "Why does this matter to me?" Consider whether these achievements align with your values or if they were motivated by external expectations.

3. **Define Success on Your Own Terms**: Using your reflections, write a new definition of success for yourself. How will you know when you're thriving? What will success feel like when it's truly aligned with who you are?

4. **Create a Plan for Aligned Success**: Finally, create a plan that focuses on pursuing success in a way that's fulfilling for you. Set goals that reflect your values and well-being, not just external metrics.

Key Takeaways:

- Traditional markers of success, such as wealth and status, often fall short of providing true fulfilment.

- Dolly Parton and Howard Schultz exemplify how success is redefined through authenticity and purpose.

- Lionel Richie's work on *We Are the World* shows the power of collective success and making an impact through collaboration.

- Redefining success means aligning with your values, setting boundaries, and focusing on the impact you make, rather than chasing external validation.

- Success should never come at the expense of your health or relationships—thriving means finding balance and fulfilment.

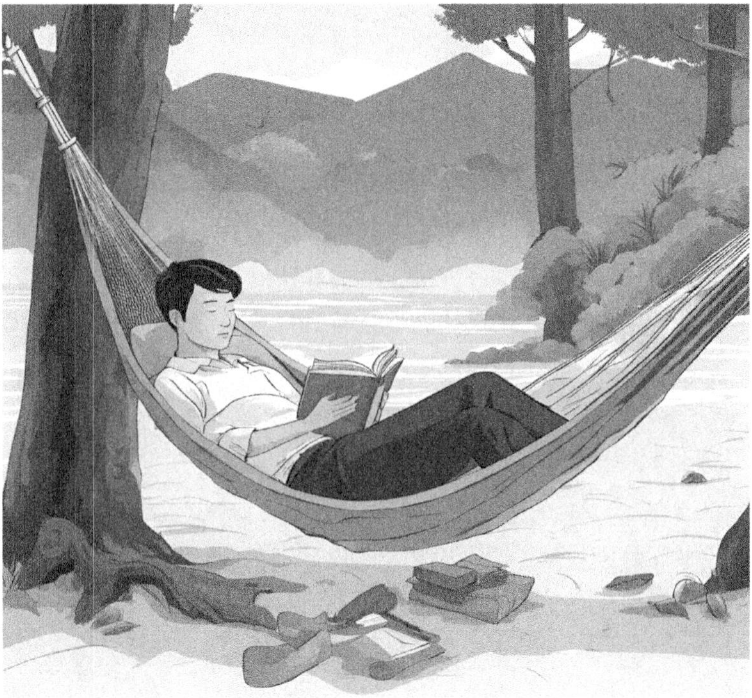

Chapter 13: Thriving Through Rest and Recovery - The Importance of Switching Off

In a world where productivity is often glorified, rest and recovery are seen as luxuries rather than necessities. We're taught to push harder, work longer hours, and always be "on." Yet, if thriving is our goal, rest and recovery aren't optional - they're essential.

The culture of hustle can lead to burnout, stress, and diminishing returns on our efforts. True thriving requires balance, and that balance can only come from recognising when it's time to switch off. Taking time to rest doesn't just prevent burnout - it boosts creativity, improves focus, and enhances overall well-being. It's through rest and recovery that we regain the energy and clarity needed to truly thrive.

In this chapter, we'll explore the importance of rest and recovery, why it's vital to switch off regularly, and practical strategies for integrating downtime into your life.

The Myth of Constant Productivity

One of the biggest misconceptions in today's culture is the idea that constant productivity equals success. In reality, our brains and bodies aren't designed to work non-stop. When we push ourselves too hard without taking time to rest, we begin to see a decline in performance, creativity, and even physical health.

The rise of remote working has blurred the lines between work and personal time. People often start earlier, work later, and don't take breaks, even for casual chats or making a coffee with a colleague. This constant connection to work makes it harder to switch off, as the boundary between work and home life becomes less clear.

However, the science behind productivity shows that working longer doesn't necessarily mean working better. When we don't give ourselves time to rest, we experience decision fatigue - the gradual depletion of mental energy that comes from making countless decisions throughout the day. This not only affects our ability to make good decisions but also reduces our creativity and problem-solving skills.

The Benefits of Rest and Recovery

Rest isn't just about taking time off - it's about giving your mind and body the space they need to recover and recharge. When we rest, we allow our brains to process information, consolidate memories, and come up with creative solutions that we might not see when we're actively focused on a problem.

Switching off also enhances our emotional well-being. Constant work without breaks leads to elevated stress levels, which can cause burnout, anxiety, and even depression. Rest allows us to reset, reduce stress, and return to our tasks with renewed focus and energy.

Rest doesn't always mean doing nothing. Activities like walking, exercising, meditating, or spending time in nature can be incredibly restorative. These activities help shift your focus away from work and give your mind the opportunity to wander, which often leads to breakthrough ideas or insights you wouldn't have come up with otherwise.

The Power of Power Naps

While sleep is often thought of as something we do only at night, power naps offer a remarkable way to recharge during the day. A power nap is a short sleep, typically lasting 10–20 minutes, designed to improve focus, alertness, and energy.

Why Power Naps Work:

- Power naps allow your brain to rest without entering deep sleep, which prevents grogginess.
- They enhance memory, learning, and cognitive function by giving your mind a short but effective reset.
- Studies have shown that a well-timed nap can boost productivity, improve mood, and reduce stress levels.

Tips for Effective Power Naps:

1. **Keep It Short:** Limit your nap to 10–20 minutes to avoid entering deep sleep, which can leave you feeling groggy.

2. **Find the Right Time:** Aim for mid-afternoon (around 1–3 PM), when natural energy levels tend to dip.

3. **Create a Restful Environment:** Nap in a quiet, dark, and comfortable space. If you're at work, consider using noise-cancelling headphones or an eye mask.

4. **Set an Alarm:** Use a timer to ensure you wake up after the ideal duration.

Power naps are a quick and accessible way to recharge during busy days, helping you maintain energy and focus without sacrificing hours.

Time Blocking: Structuring Rest into Your Day

Another practical way to ensure rest is by using time blocking - a method where you schedule specific blocks of time for focused work, breaks, and personal activities. Time blocking not only helps you structure your day but also ensures you prioritise rest as much as work.

How Time Blocking Works:

1. **Start with Priorities:** Identify your most important tasks for the day and assign them to specific time slots.

2. **Schedule Breaks and Naps:** Include short breaks every hour or two, and consider adding a power nap block in the mid-afternoon.

3. **Plan for Restorative Activities:** Set aside time for activities that recharge you, such as exercise, reading, or spending time with loved ones.

4. **Stick to Your Blocks:** Treat your rest blocks as non-negotiable appointments. When it's time to take a break, step away from work completely.

Time blocking helps create boundaries and balance. By intentionally carving out time for rest, you prevent burnout and give yourself the mental clarity needed to thrive.

Switching Off: Why It's Harder Than Ever

In today's digital age, switching off has become more difficult than ever. We're constantly bombarded with notifications, emails, and social media updates, making it hard to truly disconnect. This constant connection to technology keeps our brains in a state of heightened alertness, preventing us from fully relaxing.

Taking time to switch off - whether by going for a walk, hitting the gym, or spending time in nature - gives your mind space to clear and refocus. It's in these moments of disconnection that you often gain clarity, see the bigger picture, and return to your tasks with fresh insights and renewed energy.

The Power of Sleep in Thriving

Sleep is one of the most powerful forms of rest, yet many people underestimate its importance. Getting enough high-quality sleep is essential for maintaining cognitive function, emotional regulation, and physical health. When you're well-rested, you're more likely to make better decisions, think creatively, and handle stress effectively.

Arianna Huffington, founder of The Huffington Post and author of *The Sleep Revolution*, is a vocal advocate for the importance of sleep. After collapsing from exhaustion in 2007, Huffington realised that her relentless pursuit of success was unsustainable without adequate rest. Since then, she has become a champion for sleep and well-being, encouraging others to prioritise rest as a fundamental part of thriving.

Lionel Richie: Resting to Reignite Creativity

Lionel Richie provides another powerful example of the importance of rest and recovery in thriving. After achieving monumental success with hits like *All Night Long* and *We Are the World*, Richie found himself creatively drained and unsure of what direction to take next.

Instead of forcing himself to continue working, Richie took a step back from music, allowing himself time to rest and reflect. This period of rest not only helped him recover from burnout but also reignited his passion for music. When he eventually returned to the studio, he brought with him a renewed sense of creativity and focus, producing some of his most memorable work.

Practical Exercise: Creating Your Rest and Recovery Plan

Here's an exercise to help you integrate more rest and recovery into your routine:

1. **Assess Your Current Habits:** Reflect on how much rest and recovery you currently allow yourself. Are you getting enough sleep? Do you take regular breaks? How often do you switch off from work?

2. **Identify Areas for Improvement:** Consider where you could incorporate more rest into your routine. Maybe you need to set firmer boundaries between work and personal life, or perhaps you need to prioritise power naps or sleep.

3. **Create a Plan for Rest:** Write down one or two specific actions you'll take to ensure you get more rest and recovery. This could include scheduling breaks, adding a power nap, or planning a weekend away to recharge.

4. **Commit to Rest:** Treat rest as a priority, not an afterthought. Stick to your plan and make it an essential part of your routine.

Key Takeaways:

- Rest and recovery are essential for thriving - without them, we risk burnout, decreased productivity, and reduced creativity.

- Power naps are a quick and effective way to recharge during the day, improving focus and energy.

- Time blocking helps ensure rest and recovery are built into your daily routine.

- Prioritising sleep improves cognitive function, emotional resilience, and overall well-being.

- Switching off - whether through exercise, nature, or mindful activities - helps reset your mind and body for peak performance.

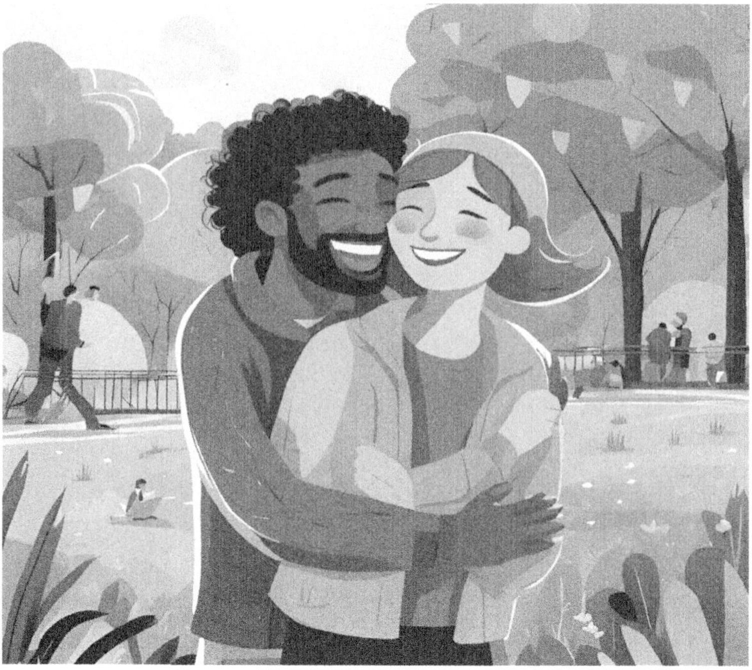

Chapter 14: Thriving in Relationships - Building Deeper Connections

At the core of thriving is the ability to cultivate meaningful, fulfilling relationships. Whether they are personal, romantic, or professional, relationships play a crucial role in our overall happiness, sense of purpose, and well-being. Thriving in relationships doesn't mean that everything will always be smooth or conflict-free, but it does mean developing the skills and emotional intelligence to navigate the challenges and deepen connections over time.

In today's fast-paced world, building deeper connections can be difficult. Social media, remote work, and busy schedules often lead to more surface-level interactions rather than meaningful connections. But the relationships we foster - whether with friends, family, colleagues, or romantic partners - are essential to thriving. In this chapter, we'll explore the power of relationships, why they matter, and how to build and sustain deeper, more fulfilling connections.

Why Relationships Matter for Thriving

Humans are wired for connection. Relationships provide us with support, companionship, and a sense of belonging. Research has shown that strong relationships are one of the most important predictors of long-term happiness and life satisfaction. In fact, the Harvard Study of Adult Development, one of the longest-running studies on happiness, found that the quality of our relationships is one of the most significant factors in determining overall well-being.

When you have strong relationships, you're more likely to be resilient in the face of challenges. You have people to turn to for support, advice, or simply a listening ear. These relationships provide emotional nourishment and help buffer against stress, making it easier to cope with difficulties and maintain a positive outlook on life.

However, thriving in relationships requires more than just surrounding yourself with people - it's about cultivating deeper, more meaningful connections that can withstand the ups and downs of life. This requires emotional intelligence, vulnerability, and an active investment in the people you care about.

The Role of Vulnerability in Deeper Connections

One of the most powerful ways to deepen your relationships is through vulnerability. Vulnerability doesn't mean exposing every detail of your life to others, but rather being open, honest, and authentic in your interactions. When you allow yourself to be vulnerable, you create an opportunity for deeper connection, trust, and understanding.

Brené Brown, a researcher and author known for her work on vulnerability and shame, argues that vulnerability is the key to meaningful relationships. According to Brown, vulnerability allows us to be seen for who we truly are, without the masks or facades we often use to protect ourselves from judgment. It's in these moments of vulnerability that true connection is built.

For example, in a professional context, vulnerability might mean admitting when you don't have all the answers or asking for help when you need it. In a romantic relationship, it might mean being honest about your fears or insecurities. In both cases, vulnerability creates an environment of trust and openness, which leads to stronger, more resilient relationships.

The Power of Empathy and Active Listening

Empathy and active listening are foundational to building deep, meaningful connections. Empathy is the ability to understand and share the feelings of another person, while active listening involves fully focusing on the person speaking, without interrupting or thinking about what you'll say next.

When you practice empathy, you demonstrate that you care about the other person's feelings and experiences. This helps build trust and emotional intimacy, whether it's in a personal relationship or a professional setting.

Oprah Winfrey is known for her exceptional ability to connect with people through empathy and active listening. Throughout her career as a talk show host, she built deep connections with her guests and audience by genuinely listening to their stories and responding with empathy. Oprah's ability to make people feel seen and heard is one of the reasons she's been able to build such meaningful, lasting relationships with those around her.

Practical Tip: How to Practice Active Listening

Next time you're in a conversation, practice active listening by doing the following:

1. **Be Present**: Put away distractions, such as your phone, and focus entirely on the person speaking.
2. **Don't Interrupt**: Resist the urge to jump in with your own thoughts or solutions. Let the other person finish before responding.
3. **Reflect Back**: Once they've finished speaking, reflect back what you've heard to show that you've been listening. For example, "It sounds like you're feeling frustrated because…"
4. **Ask Open-Ended Questions**: Encourage them to share more by asking open-ended questions like, "How did that make you feel?" or "What are you thinking about now?"

Building Trust in Relationships

Trust is the cornerstone of any strong relationship. Without trust, relationships become fragile and susceptible to breakdowns, misunderstandings, and conflicts. Building trust takes time, but it's essential for thriving in relationships. Trust is built through consistency, honesty, and vulnerability.

Keanu Reeves is known not only for his success in Hollywood but also for the deep trust he's built with those around him. Known for his humility and genuine nature, Reeves is often described by his colleagues as down-to-earth and trustworthy. He treats people with kindness, whether they're co-stars or crew members, and consistently shows up as his authentic self. This has earned him a reputation for being one of the most well-liked and trusted figures in Hollywood.

Building trust doesn't happen overnight—it's about consistently showing up for others, keeping your word, and being honest, even when it's difficult. When people know they can trust you, it strengthens the relationship and creates a solid foundation for growth and connection.

Handling Conflict with Emotional Intelligence

No relationship is without conflict. In fact, conflict can often lead to growth if handled well. The key to thriving in relationships isn't avoiding conflict altogether but learning how to navigate it with emotional intelligence.

Emotional intelligence involves recognising and managing your own emotions while being mindful of the emotions of others. When conflicts arise, it's important to stay calm, listen to the other person's perspective, and avoid reacting impulsively.

One technique for managing conflict is to focus on the issue at hand, rather than bringing up past grievances or making personal attacks. When both parties approach conflict with a mindset of resolution, rather than blame, the conflict becomes an opportunity to strengthen the relationship, rather than damage it.

Practical Tip: Managing Conflict with Emotional Intelligence

When you find yourself in a conflict, use the following steps to manage the situation effectively:

1. **Stay Calm**: Take a few deep breaths to calm your emotions before responding.
2. **Listen to Understand**: Focus on understanding the other person's perspective without interrupting or getting defensive.
3. **Express Yourself Clearly**: When it's your turn to speak, express your feelings using "I" statements, such as "I feel frustrated because…"
4. **Focus on Solutions**: Rather than dwelling on the problem, work together to find a solution that works for both parties.

Key Takeaways:

- Strong relationships are essential to happiness, resilience, and life satisfaction, providing support and a sense of belonging.
- Vulnerability allows you to build trust and deeper connections by being open, honest, and authentic in your interactions.
- Empathy and active listening help strengthen bonds by showing genuine care and understanding for others' feelings and experiences.
- Trust is built through consistent actions, honesty, and showing up authentically, creating a foundation for lasting relationships.
- Conflict, when handled with emotional intelligence, can deepen understanding and strengthen relationships over time.
- Investing time and effort in meaningful relationships helps foster deeper connections, even in a busy, digital world.

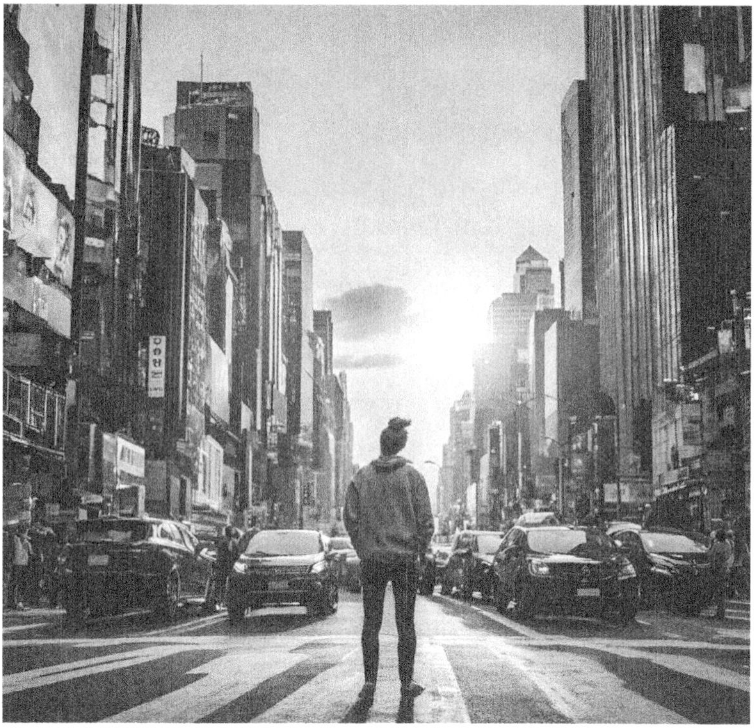

Chapter 15: The Thriving Mindset - Are You Thriving or Just Coping?

There's a subtle but significant difference between thriving and merely coping. Many of us go through life feeling busy and overwhelmed, mistaking that frenetic pace for success or growth. In reality, thriving means more than just managing day-to-day pressures - it means growing, flourishing, and finding joy in the process. It's about moving beyond survival mode to a state where you feel fulfilled, energized, and balanced.

Coping often involves doing just enough to keep things afloat - getting through each day, managing stress, and handling responsibilities. While coping is sometimes necessary, especially during challenging times, it's not sustainable in the long term if your goal is to thrive. Thriving, on the other hand, involves embracing challenges as opportunities for growth, finding purpose in what you do, and living in alignment with your values.

In this chapter, we'll explore how to shift from a coping mindset to a thriving mindset, the signs that you might be just coping, and the practical steps you can take to start truly thriving.

The Difference Between Coping and Thriving

At first glance, coping and thriving might seem similar - they both involve dealing with life's challenges. However, the two mindsets are quite different in how they approach those challenges and what the long-term outcomes are.

- **Coping** is reactive. It's about responding to challenges as they come up and doing your best to manage them. It often involves putting out fires, juggling responsibilities, and feeling like you're always one step behind. People who are coping may feel overwhelmed, stressed, or stuck in survival mode.

- **Thriving** is proactive. It's about taking control of your life, setting intentional goals, and seeing challenges as opportunities for growth. Thriving involves not just managing stress but learning from it and using it to propel you forward. People who are thriving feel energized, focused, and purposeful.

One of the key differences is the sense of control. When you're coping, you may feel like life is happening to you, and you're just trying to keep up. When you're thriving, you feel empowered to shape your own experiences, no matter what external pressures arise.

Signs You're Just Coping

It's not always easy to recognize when you're just coping, especially because it can feel like you're doing everything "right." You might be checking off tasks on your to-do list, meeting deadlines, and fulfilling responsibilities, but still not feel a sense of fulfilment. Here are some signs that you might be in coping mode rather than thriving:

- **Constant Busyness Without Fulfilment**: You're always busy, but you rarely feel a sense of accomplishment or joy in what you're doing. You're ticking off boxes but not growing or feeling energized by your work or life.

- **Feeling Overwhelmed by Stress**: Stress is a normal part of life, but if you're constantly feeling overwhelmed by it and find it difficult to relax or take breaks, you might be coping rather than thriving.

- **Lack of Purpose or Direction**: If you're moving through life without a clear sense of purpose or long-term goals, it's easy to fall into coping mode. Thriving requires having a sense of direction and working towards something meaningful.

- **Exhaustion Without Renewal**: Coping can leave you feeling drained, both physically and emotionally. If you're always tired and struggling to find energy or motivation, it's a sign that you might be in survival mode.

- **Resentment of Responsibilities**: If you feel like your work, relationships, or obligations are weighing you down rather than fulfilling you, this could be a sign that you're coping rather than thriving.

Moving from Coping to Thriving

Shifting from coping to thriving requires a change in mindset. It involves moving from a place of survival and reaction to a place of intention, growth, and purpose. Here are some practical steps to help you make that shift:

1. Clarify Your Values and Purpose

One of the first steps in moving from coping to thriving is to get clear on your values and your purpose. What matters most to you? What brings you joy and fulfilment? Take time to reflect on what drives you and use that as a compass to guide your decisions and actions.

If you find yourself caught up in tasks or responsibilities that don't align with your values, it's easy to fall into coping mode. Thriving requires living in alignment with your values and pursuing things that are meaningful to you.

Practical Exercise: Purpose Reflection Take 10 minutes each day for a week to reflect on your purpose. Ask yourself:

- What am I doing when I feel most fulfilled?
- What values do I want to prioritize in my life?
- How can I bring more of what matters to me into my daily routine?

2. Focus on Growth, Not Perfection

When you're coping, it's easy to get caught up in trying to be perfect, doing everything right and managing all your responsibilities without making mistakes. But thriving isn't about perfection; it's about growth. It's about embracing challenges as opportunities to learn and improve, rather than sources of stress.

Shifting to a growth mindset allows you to approach life's challenges with curiosity and resilience. Instead of seeing setbacks as failures, you see them as opportunities to grow stronger and wiser.

3. Set Boundaries and Prioritise Self-Care

One of the reasons people stay stuck in coping mode is because they don't set clear boundaries between their work and personal life. When you're always "on," it's impossible to truly thrive. Thriving requires making time for rest, relaxation, and self-care.

Setting boundaries means being clear about what you're willing to take on and what you need to let go of. It also means carving out time for activities that recharge you, whether that's exercising, spending time with loved ones, or simply relaxing.

Practical Tip: Use Time-Blocking to break up your workday into focused intervals, followed by short breaks. This ensures that you're taking regular pauses to rest and recharge, rather than burning out by pushing yourself too hard.

---

4. Cultivate Resilience by Embracing Discomfort

Thriving often involves stepping outside your comfort zone. While coping may involve staying in a place of safety and familiarity, thriving requires embracing challenges and learning to be comfortable with discomfort.

Building resilience doesn't mean avoiding stress - it means learning how to manage and grow from it. Dolly Parton is a perfect example of someone who has embraced discomfort and challenge to thrive. From her early struggles in the music industry to creating her own path, Parton has consistently taken risks, faced adversity with humour, and used those experiences to propel her career forward.

---

5. Practice Gratitude and Celebrate Small Wins

A key difference between coping and thriving is the ability to find joy and satisfaction in everyday life. Thriving involves recognizing and celebrating the small wins along the way, rather than waiting for big milestones to feel accomplished.

Practicing gratitude can help you shift your mindset from survival mode to a place of abundance and appreciation. By focusing on what's going well in your life and celebrating progress - no matter how small - you'll start to feel more fulfilled and energized.

Practical Exercise: Daily Gratitude At the end of each day, write down three things you're grateful for. These could be small moments of joy, accomplishments, or positive interactions. Over time, this practice will help you focus on the positive aspects of your life and cultivate a thriving mindset.

Keanu Reeves: Thriving by Staying Grounded

Keanu Reeves is a prime example of someone who has learned to thrive by staying grounded, despite the pressures of fame and the demands of his career. Reeves has consistently shown that success isn't about chasing external validation or perfection but about staying true to yourself, embracing life's ups and downs, and finding joy in the simple things.

Despite personal tragedies and the challenges of navigating Hollywood, Reeves has maintained a down-to-earth attitude, focusing on the things that bring him peace and fulfilment - whether it's through his passion for motorcycles or his dedication to supporting charitable causes. His ability to remain grounded and resilient is a powerful example of what it means to thrive in a world that often pushes us to cope.

Are You Thriving or Just Coping? A Quick Quiz

Here's a short quiz to help you assess whether you're thriving or just coping:

1. Do you feel energized and excited about your goals, or do you feel drained and overwhelmed by your responsibilities?
2. Are you actively working towards personal growth, or are you just trying to get through the day?
3. Do you feel in control of your time and decisions, or do you feel like life is happening to you?
4. Are you making time for rest and self-care, or are you constantly pushing yourself to do more?
5. Do you celebrate small wins and progress, or are you always focused on what you haven't yet achieved?

If you answered "yes" to more of the coping-related part of the questions, it might be time to take a step back and reassess your approach to thriving.

Key Takeaways:

- Coping is about survival, while thriving is about growth, purpose, and fulfilment.

- To shift from coping to thriving, it's important to clarify your values, focus on growth over perfection, and set boundaries that protect your time and energy.

- Cultivating resilience and practicing gratitude can help you move from survival mode to a thriving mindset.

- Keanu Reeves exemplifies thriving by staying grounded, embracing challenges, and finding joy in the simple things in life.

- Thriving requires intentionality - learning to celebrate progress, set boundaries, and embrace discomfort as part of the growth process.

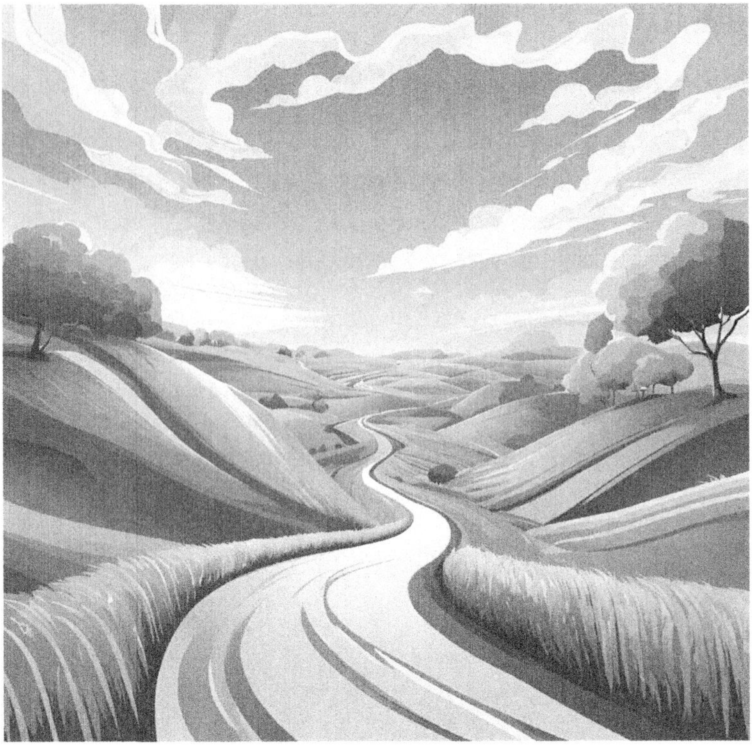

Chapter 16: Your Roadmap to Thriving - Putting It All Together

Throughout this book, we've explored the many facets of thriving - finding purpose, building resilience, fostering creativity, cultivating emotional intelligence, and developing deeper connections. Thriving isn't about perfection or constantly striving to be more productive. It's about aligning your life with your values, taking care of your well-being, and creating a sense of fulfilment that goes beyond traditional measures of success.

Now that you've taken the journey through each chapter, it's time to bring it all together. Thriving is not something that happens overnight. It's a continual process of growth, reflection, and intentional action. As you move forward, this final chapter offers a practical roadmap to help you integrate the lessons from this book into your life.

The Thriving Mindset

Before diving into the roadmap, it's important to recognize that thriving is as much about mindset as it is about action. Thriving requires a growth mindset - the belief that you can learn, improve, and evolve through challenges. It involves being open to change, embracing discomfort as a pathway to growth, and maintaining a sense of curiosity and playfulness.

As you reflect on the different aspects of thriving discussed in this book, consider how you can cultivate this mindset in your everyday life. Thriving isn't about ticking off a list of achievements; it's about continuously growing and finding joy in the process.

Your Thriving Roadmap: 5 Steps to Move Forward

Here's a practical roadmap to help you start thriving:

Step 1: Clarify Your Purpose and Values

Everything starts with purpose. Without a clear sense of what drives you, it's easy to feel lost, overwhelmed, or disconnected. Take time to revisit what you've learned about purpose in Chapter 1. Reflect on the following questions:

- What gives me a sense of meaning and fulfilment?
- How can I align my daily actions with my values?
- What long-term goals do I want to work toward, and why are they important to me?

Write down your purpose statement - something that captures what you want your life to stand for. This will serve as your compass for making decisions, setting goals, and staying focused on what truly matters.

Step 2: Build Resilience Through Rest and Recovery

As we explored in Chapters 6 and 13, resilience is a key component of thriving. But resilience doesn't come from constant hustle - it comes from balance. The ability to bounce back from challenges requires rest and recovery.

Create a plan for incorporating regular rest into your routine. This might include:

- Scheduling regular downtime in your calendar.
- Practicing task batching and time-blocking during your workday to ensure you take breaks.
- Prioritising sleep and making sure you're getting the rest you need to recharge.

Without rest, you're more likely to fall into survival mode, focusing on coping rather than thriving. Make rest a non-negotiable part of your thriving plan.

Step 3: Develop Emotional Intelligence and Deep Connections

Thriving isn't just about individual success - it's about building meaningful relationships and navigating emotions with skill. In Chapter 9, we explored how emotional intelligence (EI) helps you thrive by improving self-awareness, empathy, and emotional regulation. Chapter 14 delved into the importance of building deep connections through trust, vulnerability, and active listening.

Start by practicing self-awareness. Make it a daily habit to check in with yourself and ask, "How am I feeling?" Name your emotions, as we discussed in Chapter 9, to reduce their intensity and help you respond thoughtfully rather than react impulsively.

Next, focus on strengthening your connections with others. Relationships are the foundation of thriving, and they require time, attention, and vulnerability. Take a step this week to deepen an important relationship - whether it's by being more present, sharing your true feelings, or actively listening.

Step 4: Embrace Creativity and Playfulness

In Chapters 8 and 10, we learned that thriving requires more than hard work - it requires creativity and playfulness. Tapping into your creative side and allowing yourself to have fun are essential to maintaining balance, finding innovative solutions, and staying energized.

Find ways to bring creativity and playfulness into your life. This might be through hobbies, experimenting with new approaches to problems, or simply allowing yourself time to explore new interests without the pressure of "succeeding." Remember, Dolly Parton's creativity and playful spirit were key to her long-lasting success.

Make it a habit to incorporate playfulness into your daily life, whether through playful brainstorming sessions, trying new hobbies, or simply making time for fun and joy.

Step 5: Continuously Reflect and Adjust

Thriving is not a one-time achievement - it's a continuous process of reflection and growth. As you move forward, make it a habit to regularly reflect on your progress and adjust as needed. Ask yourself:

- Am I living in alignment with my values and purpose?
- What's working well in my life, and what needs adjustment?
- How can I continue to grow, both personally and professionally?

This reflection will help you stay on track, ensure that you're not slipping back into coping mode, and allow you to make any necessary changes to keep thriving.

Thriving Progress Review: Where Are You Now?

As you finish this book, it's time to pause and reflect on how far you've come. Thriving isn't a one-time achievement - it's a lifetime journey. This Thriving Progress Review will help you assess where you are now and identify areas for growth. The journey doesn't end here - return to these questions in the future to keep track of your evolving goals and mindset. Remember, thriving is about continuous growth, not perfection.

Take a moment to answer these questions:

1. **Purpose**: Have you clarified your purpose? Are you working toward goals that align with your values?
2. **Rest**: Are you making time for rest and recovery, or are you constantly pushing yourself to do more?
3. **Emotional Intelligence**: How are you handling your emotions? Are you practicing self-awareness and empathy in your relationships?
4. **Creativity**: Are you giving yourself time to experiment, play, and be creative?
5. **Connections**: How are your relationships? Are you building deep, meaningful connections with others?

As life evolves, make a habit of revisiting these questions. Your thriving journey is ongoing—check in with yourself regularly to ensure you're staying aligned with your purpose and values.

Your Call to Action: Play, Experiment, Share

As you continue your journey toward thriving, remember that thriving isn't a solo endeavour. It's about playing, experimenting, and sharing what you've learned with others.

1. Play

Make time for play - whether it's through hobbies, creative projects, or simply having fun with friends and family. Playfulness keeps you open to new possibilities and helps you stay energized and joyful, even during challenging times.

2. Experiment

Experiment with new ways of thinking, working, and living. Don't be afraid to try new approaches, take risks, and learn from your experiences. As you experiment, you'll discover what works best for you and how you can continue to grow and evolve.

3. Share

Finally, don't keep what you've learned to yourself. Share your experiences with others—whether it's by discussing the concepts in this book, supporting a friend in their journey to thrive, or even creating a community around the idea of thriving.

As Lionel Richie demonstrated with *We Are the World*, sometimes the greatest impact comes from working together. Sharing your journey not only helps you grow but also inspires others to do the same.

Thriving is a Journey, Not a Destination

Thriving is not a final destination - it's a journey. It's about consistently growing, evolving, and finding balance in all areas of life. There will be times when you face setbacks, challenges, and moments where you feel like you're back in coping mode. That's normal. The key is to remain intentional, reflect on what's working, and continue moving forward with a thriving mindset.

As you finish this book, I encourage you to take everything you've learned and put it into practice. Don't just read about thriving - live it. Play, experiment, share, and grow. Thriving is within your reach, and it's a journey worth taking.

Enjoy your journey.

Afterword

I feel that we each underestimate our ability to thrive and this potentially restricts us from taking action, making plans and living life to its fullest potential.

So that you truly appreciate your ever-increasing ability to thrive, I recommend you use the following pages to give yourself some recognition for your successes and learn to recognise your own strengths. Once you fully understand your strengths, then you can continue to apply the over and over again.

Here's to your ongoing success....

January 2025

Challenges or struggles I've faced this month are...

Strengths, tools and techniques I've used to help me thrive are...

February 2025

Challenges or struggles I've faced this month are...

Strengths, tools and techniques I've used to help me thrive are...

March 2025

Challenges or struggles I've faced this month are...

Strengths, tools and techniques I've used to help me thrive are...

April 2025

Challenges or struggles I've faced this month are...

Strengths, tools and techniques I've used to help me thrive are...

May 2025

Challenges or struggles I've faced this month are...

Strengths, tools and techniques I've used to help me thrive are...

June 2025

Challenges or struggles I've faced this month are...

Strengths, tools and techniques I've used to help me thrive are...

July 2025

Challenges or struggles I've faced this month are...

Strengths, tools and techniques I've used to help me thrive are...

August 2025

Challenges or struggles I've faced this month are...

Strengths, tools and techniques I've used to help me thrive are...

September 2025

Challenges or struggles I've faced this month are...

Strengths, tools and techniques I've used to help me thrive are...

October 2025

Challenges or struggles I've faced this month are...

Strengths, tools and techniques I've used to help me thrive are...

November 2025

Challenges or struggles I've faced this month are...

Strengths, tools and techniques I've used to help me thrive are...

December 2025

Challenges or struggles I've faced this month are...

Strengths, tools and techniques I've used to help me thrive are...

Printed in Great Britain
by Amazon